# The Equation of Sales

## A Practical Guide to Selling Technology

## Tim Gibbons

Shield Crest

© Copyright 2021 Tim Gibbons

All rights reserved

ISBN: 978-1-913839-19-2

MMXXI

A CIP catalogue record for this book is available from the British Library

Published by
ShieldCrest Publishing Ltd.,
Aylesbury, Buckinghamshire,
HP18 0TF England
Tel: +44 (0) 333 8000 890
www.shieldcrest.co.uk

To Claire, Robbie and Izzy

*"I love you with all the madness in my soul"* (\*)

## Disclaimer

The material in this book is of the nature of general comment only and does not represent professional advice. It is not intended to provide specific guidance for particular circumstances and it should not be relied on as the basis for any decision to take action or not take action on any matter which it covers. Readers should obtain professional advice where appropriate before making any such decision. To the maximum extent permitted by law, the author and publisher disclaim all responsibility and liability to any person, arising directly or indirectly from any person taking or not taking action based on the information in this publication.

# CONTENTS

**EXAMPLES AND EXERCISES**

**EXTRAS**

# THANKS AND ACKNOWLEDGEMENTS

This book could not have been written without the help of many people to whom I will always be very grateful.

Robbie Gibbons, Richard Jefferies and John Powter who read the whole book and provided great ideas and guidance.

Alan Foum, Chris Harvey, Nathan Ceglar, Mark Dorn, Andrea D'Silva, Peter Butterworth, Carmen Fraticelli, Joanne Cranswick, Max Harper, Robert Dean, Ewa Ginal, Aaron Lockwood, Gavin Elliott, Nick Tranter, Stephen Rippington, Gareth Smith, Michael Hayes, Aonghus O'Carroll, Jo Reid, Lucy Plant, Sean Akinwale, Dave Waters, Nick Reilly, Colin Clarke, Philipa Tolley, James Bargeron, Elizabeth Desser, Kashif Saeed, Rafique Samdani, Victoria Belan, Alex Kurobasa , Antony Biondi, Chris Pettit, Yusuf Keskin and Imran Ali all of whom read a chapter and provided me with the belief that I was not writing utter drivel.

Jane Crump of Foreshaw Design for designing the front and back covers.

Lots of people, too numerous to mention, with whom I have worked over many years and who have provided stories, ideas and experiences that have all been brought together into the book.

Everyone I have trained over the last five years for their inspiration, stories and feedback which has further shaped my ideas. Also to their management for trusting me to be able to train their teams.

Finally, to my family, Claire, Robbie, Izzy and Rocky for their support and encouragement since I started the business. Thanks for never telling me to get a proper job!

# ABOUT THE AUTHOR

Tim has over 30 years of experience in industry, particularly the oil and gas industry. He has a BA in Physics from University of Oxford and a MSc in Exploration Geophysics from Imperial College, London. He has worked for both oil companies and service companies so has experienced work as both a buyer and a seller.

Tim has over 20 years of sales and commercial experience gained with three major technology companies. He held a variety of managerial, sales and business development roles in each organisation demonstrating an ability to grow the business he was responsible for in all cases. He has experience of selling computing technology, data and services in Europe, Africa and Australia.

In 2015, Tim founded Hoolock Consulting to provide sales consulting and training to technology and engineering companies based on The Equation of Sales. Building trust with customers, understanding their needs and articulating the value of the products he is supplying are the cornerstones of his approach.

"Tim is a sales rock star especially when it comes to building trust and coaching clients. His technical expertise combined with business experience is second to none." Merv Swan, a former Halliburton Executive.

# READER COMMENTS

*"One of a few books that set out the sale processes in an articulate manner. Aimed at selling technology and technical services for those new to sales or a great reference to any seasoned sales manager. More than worthy of a place on your desk."*

Peter Butterworth, Business Development Manager

*"This book is great at explaining the sales process to non-sales people, this enables non sales colleagues to understand their salespeople and to work more effectively with them in order to achieve business results"*

Alan Foum, Consultant Geophysicist.

*"The Equation of Sales is clearly written by someone with years at the sharp end, and real life experience of what does and doesn't work. It's a book that should be read, not only by those taking their first steps on the Sales path, but also those of us with worn soles, as there are a lot of truths hidden in these pages. And if you fancy a career as an archetypal second hand car salesman, this book probably isn't for you."*

Andrew Gallacher, European Actuarial Lead Partner

*"I am a mere 17 pages in to 'The Equation of Sales' and where it is clearly foundational and baseline instructive for new sales professionals in tech, the messaging is clear, concise and dead on. Refreshingly good."*

Rob Dudley, Senior Vice President, Global Sales

*"Anyone involved in sales should have a copy of this book, equally suited to those setting out on a sales career and experienced professionals. It is full of sales insight, practical advice and actionable tools for all sales professionals"*

Dr Aaron Lockwood, Software Sales Manager

*"An interesting and informative guide to the sales process. Highly recommended."*

Chris Pettit, Managing Director, KeyFacts Energy.

# INTRODUCTION

*"I never lose. I either win or learn."*

Nelson Mandela

When I was writing this book, I asked a number of people to read and review it so that I knew whether I was writing anything useful or not. A few of them asked me what I thought was different about this book compared to any other, what made it unique such that people would want to buy it. It is a very difficult question to answer as there are so many sales books already available; over 60,000 on Amazon.

So, why should you read this book?

Firstly, this book is about selling technology and technical services. There are actually very few sales book about this. However, if you are able to sell one type of product, you probably know enough to be able to sell a different type of product in a completely different industry. Sales methods do not change much from industry to industry.

Indeed, sales methods change very little from book to book. I have read quite a number over the years and while I will learn something from all of them, there is an awful lot of repetition from one book to another. The sales process does not really change. Terminology and emphasis may change but the process is fairly constant.

When I first had a sales job, I was extremely lucky that the company I worked for was investing heavily in their sales teams and was providing us with lots of training. It felt like I was in a training class every other week. I was also lucky to be working with very experienced sales people who taught me a huge amount. However, no one ever really joined the dots for me, explaining how all these activities linked together into a coherent process.

Following the sales process is important but there are so many other things to be done, such as prioritising customers, gaining the trust of those customers, using insights to generate interest from new customers and understanding why a customer should choose our products. I learnt many things but not in any sensible order nor with any idea of a bigger picture.

So, this book is mainly aimed at people starting their careers in technology sales. It provides you with the basic tools to decide which customers to try to sell to, how to find out what they might need and how to persuade them that your product is the most effective one. For people who have been working in sales for a number of years, the book provides great tips and hints and refreshes your knowledge about these things. I am not suggesting that it is the only sales book you will ever want to buy but it should be the first sales book that you buy. It provides the foundation for further training and development.

The book is about how to start selling effectively so that you can make the most of your career in sales. I am not sure if it is my age or general character, but I get very grumpy when people make very little effort when trying to sell to me. However, I have also learnt enough to know that it is probably not their fault. They have not been taught to do it properly.

I have had estate agents show me around a house and never once ask me what was important to me about the home that I wanted to buy. I have had cold callers launch straight into their script without ever asking if I even had the time to listen to them. I have had car sellers go straight into the finance of the deal without ever checking if I knew enough about the car to make an informed decision. None of these are the best way to go about selling and I believe that this book can help to change those poor processes.

I am firmly of the belief that sales is actually quite easy. Make a product, find someone who wants to buy it and sell it to them for a price that makes sense for both of you. The problem is that most people, myself included, have a tendency to forget the basics. We have multiple products to sell to multiple customers; we have quotas to meet and expectations to manage. Juggling everything is difficult and as a result, we do not always work in the most effective way.

In keeping with the idea that sales is easy, I have tried to keep this book as straight forward as possible. Since each company will have its own sales process and each product will have its own features and benefits, it is not possible to be too prescriptive. I have written about the basic activities that a sales person must do in order to be effective and efficient. You will have to take these and apply them to your company, your processes and your products. You also require time to apply them to your work. I suggest adopting a couple of ideas at a time; improve these aspects of your work and then move on to the next ideas. If you try to change everything at once, you may struggle to be successful.

While obviously this is a book, I believe that it can be difficult to learn sales just by reading a book. Sales is an activity and you have to do it in order to get better. As a teenager, I tried to improve my golf game by reading a book. I lay in bed at night trying to understand how to swing my arms and rotate my hips from plain text and no diagrams! Suffice to say, I did not get much better. Sales is the same. It is an activity that you must read, understand and then practise.

The book is just the first step in improving your sales skills. It provides you with background knowledge and ideas but you need to put them into practise. This is why it includes worked examples using a fictitious technology company and a series of activity sheets. These are there so that you can immediately apply these lessons to your own products and customers.

You will require time and space to work on your skills and continue to apply the lessons from the book to your weekly and monthly activities. The examples will provide you with ideas to get you started; the exercises will help you to apply them to your products. Beyond that, there are online and in-person training courses that can be provided that will add a layer of experience to your knowledge.

There are further sales activities that require other people to be involved, such as questioning and active listening. For these, you should seek the help of colleagues in order to practise. You have to practise in order to get better. Every professional sports person trains and practises. It should be no different for a professional sales person. Only with constant practise can you get better over time. I strongly urge you to take the time to work with others to improve your skills.

I have written this book to support the work of a single sales person. In reality, sales people work as a team with a wide variety of people contributing to the process. The sales person is not always responsible for every aspect of the sales process, different people will do different things. This will vary by company and product.

One of the most significant groups that sales works with is marketing and this collaboration is getting stronger. Marketing is extremely important as it positions your company in the market place and makes potential customers aware of your products. Marketing can be very effective at driving customers towards sales by generating leads to follow up. However, it is generic and is not focussed on a specific customer.

Sales is an activity that is targeted at a specific customer. It focusses on just those customers who you believe are most likely to buy your product. It understands their specific needs and why they might be interested to buy your product to develop an opportunity. Sales is then about developing those opportunities into closed deals. This is the focus of this book.

Throughout the book I mostly refer to the sale of products. In reality, this may mean products, services or the combination of both into a solution. I have used "product" simply because it is easy and most technology can be seen as a product. If you sell technical services, or prefer to refer to solutions, this book is still relevant to you. It is just a question of choice of language.

I hope that you enjoy the book and find it useful. For further follow up, Hoolock Consulting provides consulting and training on everything that is covered in the book and more. Please contact us if you would like some further help.

# 1

## THE EQUATION OF SALES

*"Someone told me that each equation I included in the book would halve the sales"*
Stephen Hawking, A Brief History of Time

**Trust x Needs x Value = Successful Selling**

When I started my sales training business, I had no real coherent structure to my training. I built all of the materials myself from experience, ideas and comments from former colleagues. When I looked at other training organisations, I saw that they always had a unifying theme that their training was built around. I realised that I had to have something that succinctly captured my ideas about sales and that I could use throughout my work.

I was thinking about all of this on the train one day when the idea of the Equation of Sales came to me rather out of the blue. I was thinking about what summed up my philosophy about sales and the three words, Trust, Needs and Value did just that. I then thought about how I could arrange them and an equation felt like the right approach. I have a background in science and technology and many of my customers provide technology or engineering solutions so an equation would be a natural thing for them to understand. From that, The Equation of Sales was born.

Trust, needs and value are the three things that a sales person has to establish with any buyer, whether they are selling shoes or aeroplanes. People buy from people that they trust; people buy something that they need and they buy something that they perceive as valuable. If the sales person cannot establish all three, generally in that order, then they will struggle to sell. Let us examine each of them in turn.

**Trust**

When I first came to live in the town where I currently live, I did not really know anyone who lived there. However, I had to employ a builder for some work on the house that I had bought. As I did not know anyone, I could not ask for recommendations. As a result, I had to contact a number of builders and ask them to come around to have a look at what was required. Eventually I found one who seemed trustworthy and gave him the work. I used him for three of four more jobs over the next few years as he did a good job and was reliable. I trusted him.

Having a recommendation can shorten the process of finding a reliable tradesman. There are now a number of schemes for providing feedback on all sorts of trades so that companies or individuals can build a profile that demonstrates that they can be trusted. Asking friends and colleagues is another good way of finding trustworthy people to work for you. Most companies when they are recruiting will offer incentives to their own staff for them to recommend someone that they know to fill a vacancy. This is not to provide extra benefits to their staff but to shorten the recruitment process and provide more certainty that they will be employing someone that is capable of doing the job.

It is almost impossible to do anything now without being asked for a review. Any purchase is followed by an email asking for a review; any hotel stay or meal out that was booked online comes with a request for a review. Whole websites and businesses exist just from online reviews. If we want to buy anything, we can find a review of it. All of these things are done to try to persuade people to trust the business that is supplying the product or service.

> If we want someone to buy from us, we first have to ask them to trust us.

So, if we want someone to buy from us, we first have to demonstrate that they can trust us. This does not happen overnight. Walking in off the street and expecting to be trusted is not likely to happen. The customer has to know that what you are offering is the right product for them and that it will do what they need it to do. They only have your word for it to start with so they must trust you before they progress.

Chapters 5 to 10 of this book cover the aspects of a sales person's role that deal with trust. They are:

Chapter 5 - Building trust, how do you go about doing this?

Chapter 6 - Why do you do what you do?

Chapter 7 - Customer Research, how to find out about your customer;

Chapter 8 - What does a good customer look like? – and which are the best ones to focus on?

Chapter 9 - How to get through the front door, what can you say to get your potential customer interested in your product?

Chapter 10 – Presentations, how to present your product in the best possible way.

## Needs

Who has not stood in line at a petrol station and thought, "You know what, I need a chocolate bar right now!" The bars are put next to the tills for exactly that reason. We do not really need the bar but we see it there and it makes us think that we need it.

How many people in business do you think make impulse buys? I do not believe that it is very many. The decision to buy a product is generally influenced by a number of people in different roles and the buying process is often controlled by a procurement department. As a result, impulse buys in a business are very infrequent. A business will have to need the product before they will buy it. You must find those needs and position your product as the solution to them.

For the customer, the process starts from having a problem or an issue, something that needs to be solved. Surveys suggest that half of all potential customers for your product will be quite happy with their current situation, they do not have a need. That is a reasonable place to be. On a personal level, we need to buy food on a regular basis but we don't need to buy an oven to cook it in quite so regularly. Our need for food is driven by our need for energy; our need for a new oven will probably come from the old one breaking down.

> Your customer will not want your product until they know that they have a need for it.

Likewise, your customer will not come to you until they perceive that they have a need. It could be as simple as they have a new employee so need to buy them a new laptop. However, it could be much more complex like being unable to track orders through their purchasing system. The new laptop is generally easy to solve and can be done quite quickly. Fixing the problems with a purchasing system requires much more information before it can be solved.

Asking questions is at the root of finding out about needs. A sales person must ask their customer about what they are doing, what they are trying to achieve and what is stopping them from achieving it. It is important to fully understand all of their needs, even those that you cannot help with or seem small and irrelevant. If they are affecting your customer, then they are affecting your ability to help them and therefore make a sale.

Chapters 11 to 13 cover the aspects of a sales person's role that deal with needs. They are:

Chapter 11 – Needs Analysis, how to uncover basic needs so that you can initiate discussions;

Chapter 12 – Asking Questions, how to ask good questions so that you can find the information that you need;

Chapter 13 – Active Listening, how to listen effectively so that you understand everything that your customer is telling you.

**Value**

The last element of the equation is value. No matter what you are buying, you have to believe that you are going to get value from it. If you have a meal in a restaurant, there are two levels of value you can receive. First, the simple act of eating provides you with sustenance and nourishment to keep going for the next few hours. However, any food can do this. The real value in a meal out is in the experience, which can include the taste of the food, ambience of the restaurant, the service, the company etc. All of this is difficult to put a price on and therefore equally difficult to value. Two different people can easily value the same experience quite differently.

In any business scenario, there is the same requirement to evaluate the value of any deal. This is easy if it is a case of buying and selling shares, if you make more money than you spend, it is good value. However, buying a new laptop for an existing employee is more difficult to define. Are they that much more productive with the new laptop? Can they do things that they could not do before hand? For the sales person, defining the value of a potential sale to a customer can be very difficult. They must think like the customer, understand the customer's exact needs and be able to translate their product's features into value for the customer.

> The customer must believe that they are going to be better off having bought your product than if they had not.

Value does not have to be measured purely in monetary terms. It could involve reduced risk; for example, replacing some equipment in an assembly line with another which breaks down less frequently will reduce the risk that the assembly line will be stopped for repairs. It could involve higher productivity; for example, replacing three machines with one which does the same job in half the time. While there is a cost involved in the purchase of the equipment, it is small compared to the savings gained by increasing productivity or increasing uptime of an assembly line. All of these demonstrate value but if the customer cannot understand how they will gain that value, they are not going to be convinced to buy the solution.

Value is very much in the eye of the person spending the money. The role of the sales person is to demonstrate clearly that their product offers value. This could involve demonstrating how it has provided value to other customers or by allowing the customer to have a trial of the product.

Chapters 14 to 21 cover the aspects of a sales person's role that deal with value. They are:

Chapter 14 – Value selling, how do you define the value of your product;

Chapter 15 – Why change? Why should your customer change what they are currently doing?

Chapter 16 – Why are you unique? What is unique about your product that is valuable to the customer?

Chapter 17 – What does a good opportunity look like? How to rank each of your opportunities to know which to focus on;

Chapter 18 – Different Buyers, how to manage all of the different people involved in the sale;

Chapter 19 – Proposals, how to write effective proposals that convince your customer to buy;

Chapter 20 – Negotiation, how to handle the negotiations required once your customer wants to buy.

Chapter 21 – Closing, how to finalise the deal and get paid.


The Equation of Sales neatly summarises the three things that a sales person has to do to convince a customer to buy from them. They must earn the trust of their customer, they must be selling a product that the customer needs and they have to demonstrate that the customer will gain value from it. It really is that simple. A lot of people will try to complicate the process or introduce lots of jargon but trust, needs and value are the three keys to a sale.

# THE SALES PROCESS

# 2

# THE SALES PROCESS

*"If you can't describe what you are doing as a process, you don't know what you're doing."*

W. Edwards Deming

**M**ost people who are new to sales often do not realise that there is a process that is generally followed. Their experience of selling has involved watching a presentation of some new technology followed by it arriving on their desk. They never saw the rest of the work that was done, the research done to identify them as a potential customer, the initial meetings with senior management to understand needs, the development of a proposal and the negotiations to close the deal.

> Sales is a process and missing out steps in that process generally leads to failure.

Sometimes our customers might take away the requirement for one stage, such as coming and asking to buy something, but even in these cases, you should be trying to follow the process as much as possible. This is particularly true if the customer approaches you. Always ask why they need your product. This is extremely useful information to ensure that you end up with a happy customer. You should also not assume that your customer understands the product completely just because they have asked to buy it.

Most books about sales are organised in a linear way according to the linear sales process that they are defining. However, the reality is that the process is not always linear. Sometimes it is necessary to loop back through the process and repeat steps. In addition, being mindful of activities required in later stages helps to define the right course of action early in the process. As a result, this book is written about activities that may happen across multiple stages of the process with the aim of getting these done effectively and efficiently.

It is important to be mindful of the overall process but not to be too driven by it. Some sales organisations implement a very complicated sales process, trying to cover every possible eventuality that their sales team may face. I believe that we should try to keep things as simple as possible and have a simple sales process that is straightforward to follow.

This is about the simplest sales process that you can follow:

Figure 2.1: The Sales Process

We will now look at each stage of the sales process and see how it relates to The Equation of Sales.

**Customer Research**

In this stage, we want to find our potential customers. For products that are sold into a vertical marketplace, like the oil industry or financial services, it is quite easy to list out all of the potential customers we might be able to sell to. For products in a horizontal marketplace, we have a much wider potential market and there may be no limit to the customers we can try to sell to.

> Sales people have to focus on the customers who are most likely to need their products.

The aim of our research is to understand some basic facts about our customers in order to determine their suitability for our product.

For example, if you are selling a technology that runs in the cloud, you want to try to find customers who are already running other technologies in the cloud. This doesn't mean that all other companies are not potential customers but they will be harder to persuade to adopt your technology because you first have to persuade them to work in the cloud before you can persuade them to buy your product.

The information that we are looking for should be the same for each company. This allows us to rank the companies against each other to define an order in which we want to approach the companies. The company that we judge to be most likely to buy should be the one that we approach first.

We discuss this stage in
Chapter 7, Customer Research and
Chapter 8, What does a good customer look like?

**Needs Analysis**

As defined in The Equation of Sales, no one buys something unless they need it. Our customer research defines our potential customers but not all customers will have an immediate, specific need that your product can satisfy.

> Not all customers will need your product today.

Our initial research is about trying to find the best potential customers for our product. We should understand what our product does and what generic value it provides to our customers. At this stage, it is just a generic value as we do not know the specific needs of each customer.

It is not always possible to see all of the needs that a customer has or the specific need that will drive them to buy your product. You may have to look for indications or suggestions that they need your product. For example, no one ever publicly states that they need sales training, so you must look for other signals that they might need it. These signals might be:

- A new sales manager
- Launch of a new product
- Declining revenues

The signals are never likely to be immediately obvious. However, there may be times when you can find specific information that is relevant to you. For example, many companies will make corporate presentations and will often acknowledge, or imply, some specific needs in these.

During your research, you may discover needs that your products cannot satisfy. It is important to be aware of these as they may be more important to your customer than the needs that you can help with. If this is the case, then your customer may not be interested in talking to you until they have resolved these more important needs. You may have to accept this and come back when it is more appropriate. Do not try to force your product on them until they are ready for it.

We discuss this in more detail in Chapter 11, Needs Analysis.

**Validation**

Based on your research, you hopefully have an idea that your customer is right for you and that they have some needs that would influence a purchase. However, you can never be sure that this is the case. You must go to talk to them to validate these ideas to be sure that this is all correct.

Even if your customer approaches you and asks to buy your product, this is still a stage that you should go through. You have to understand what is driving their request to ensure that you are proposing the right product and possibly whether you can expand the deal. The understanding of their needs will also be helpful once you go to the later stages of the sales process and negotiate the final commercial arrangement.

Validation is about asking questions of the customer. You have to understand their needs in great detail, not only to find the right product but to also determine the value that they will get from the product. This will allow you to determine the price to charge for it and will definitely help you in your negotiations.

> Validation is about asking questions of the customer to understand their needs and the value that they will get from your product.

Validation is about asking the right questions which means initially asking open questions that encourage the customer to talk. Talk about one aspect of the problem at a time and understand that fully before you move on to another. You must also actively listen. This means that you must listen carefully and demonstrate to the speaker that you are listening to them. This will ensure that you understand everything that you require in order to develop your proposal.

We discuss this in more detail in Chapter 12, Asking Questions and Chapter 13, Active Listening.

**Proposal**

Once we have met with the customer, understood their needs and how we can help them, we now have to define what we are going to actually do for them. This is documented in a proposal.

Too many companies treat the proposal like a quotation, simply listing a number of products and a price. They may pad it out with a description of the products but the proposal is entirely focussed on their company and not the customer. This is the wrong approach.

> The proposal is part of the sales process and must sell the product.

The proposal must sell the product. This is because the proposal may be read by more people than you have met with. They may be unaware of your product before they see the proposal. As a result, your proposal must be a sales document and be understandable to anyone who reads it.

To achieve this, the writer must remember why they are writing it in the first place. The customer has a need and has to understand how the products referenced in the proposal will help them to fix their need. This means that the proposal must focus on the customer and their need before ever referencing the product. Every element of the product must be referenced to the need it is helping to resolve with a clear statement of the benefit of having it. This must be a benefit or value, not a feature. Again, too many people confuse these. For example, a feature of a smart phone is that you can access emails when you are away from your desk. The benefit of this is that you can save time by responding to emails quicker than you otherwise might be able to.

We discuss this in more detail in Chapter 14, Value Selling and Chapter 19, Proposals.

## Presentation

Most people are surprised to see presentation so late in the process. They typically think that the presentation comes near the start. However, there are two types of presentations.

A marketing presentation is delivered early in the sales process and is designed to provide the customer with an overview of the products that you are offering. It generally focusses on the seller and their products with general statements of benefits. The purpose of this is to help to build trust with the customer and to initiate a conversation about their needs. Improving the customer's understanding of the products on offer usually helps with this discussion. However, too many people fail to discuss the customer's needs at this stage, they make the presentation and walk away. They then wonder why the customer never buys their product!

A sales presentation comes nearer the end of the sales process and is essentially a verbal delivery of the proposal. The sales presentation is entirely focussed on the customer and must state what is in the proposal. It is a chance for the customer to ask relevant questions and for the seller to move them towards a close. It may also include more proof of the products being sold, for example a software demonstration or a visit to a laboratory.

> A sales presentation is entirely focussed on the customer.

By the end of the presentation, the seller should be confident that the customer completely understands their solution and the benefits that it will bring to them, related directly to their needs. If all has gone well, then they should be asking to buy immediately. If not, they may start to negotiate.

We discuss presentations in more detail in Chapter 10, Presentations.

## Negotiation

If your client starts to negotiate with you, then you should be confident that you have done a good job and they want to buy your product.

People don't generally negotiate with you unless they actually want to buy. Otherwise, they would just be wasting everyone's time and that is not usually something people want to do. Wasting time or delaying may be a negotiating tactic but it is still part of the negotiation. At this point, both you and your customer should be working towards the same end – a successful sale / purchase – as that is what you both want.

> People don't generally negotiate with you unless they actually want to buy.

There are lots of reasons why a customer might want to negotiate and not all of them are related to the product or the need being satisfied. Negotiations are conducted by people and personal motivations and character come into play. To try to eliminate these problems, the seller must ensure that they understand as much as they can about the customer and their needs before they ever get into the negotiation.

In good negotiations, both sides are focussed on ensuring that they both come away with an acceptable agreement. This means that each side will trade items that are important to them in order to receive something in return. It is critical that both sides trade rather than one side giving things away or demanding that the other side gives up something for nothing. That is not a win-win situation.

For example, if the product being sold has a fixed specification, such as a software programme, then the two main variables in the deal are the price that it is sold for and the timing of the deal. A company may offer a reduction in the price in return for a quick sale. The customer benefits from the lower price and the seller benefits from the faster sale.

At the end of the negotiations, both sides should be happy with the whole agreement. It should also be the final agreement. If it is not the final agreement, then negotiations are not over!

We discuss negotiations in more detail in Chapter 20, Negotiations.

**Closing**

Closing is often considered to be the hardest part of the sales process. However, I believe that it is the easiest, provided that you have done everything well before you get there!

All that is really required to close the deal is that the relevant parties sign the agreement, in whatever format it takes. Sometimes several people are required to sign it. Sometimes several departments might be involved and each will have to be happy with the agreement before they are ready to sign. Knowing who has to sign and where they will be on the day that the deal is signed is often crucial for deals that have a time constraint on them. The sales person must be aware of all of these things as the agreement gets closer to signature.

> Closing is the easiest part of the sales process, provided that you have done everything correctly before you get there.

At the end of the negotiations, both sides should be happy with the agreement and be ready to sign it. If they are not, then you are not ready to close. Too many people try to close a deal too soon. This may be before the customer has decided to buy or even recognised the need for the product. The buyer may have to consult with colleagues rather than making the decision themselves. This is often why the sales person thinks that closing is difficult.

However, if you have done everything correctly, asking for signature and the money should be straight forward.

We discuss closing in more detail in Chapter 21, Closing.

Frequently, all of the activities in the sales process will be going on all at the same time with lots of customers. While researching one customer, you may be presenting a proposal to another and negotiating with a third. It can be difficult to keep all of the processes going at the same time while finding new opportunities to develop. There is a tendency to focus on existing opportunities at the expense of creating new ones.

To avoid this, I recommend that you set aside part of every week for Customer Research and Needs Analysis. It is very important to continue to find new opportunities. The sales process exercise at the end of the book will help with this. This will also help you to build your sales process using the most relevant and useful activities.

# 3

## BUILDING A SALES PROCESS

*"It is not the beauty of a building you should look at; it is the construction of the foundation that will stand the test of time."*
David Allan Coe.

It is likely that when you start in a new sales role, the sales process for your organisation will be already defined. However, this is probably much like the process defined above. It does not really tell you what to do on a day to day basis. The remainder of this book will provide you with ideas of what to do and why you should do them. However, as this book is designed for everyone, those ideas are somewhat generic. You will need to define specific activities that are relevant to your company, the product that you are selling and the target market.

As you do this, you will find it easier if you categorise the activities into a very simple, four stage, sales process.

Stage 1 – Suspect – I think that there might be an opportunity.
Stage 2 – Prospect – I know that there is an opportunity
Stage 3 – Opportunity – I have made the customer a proposal
Stage 4 – Sale – I have closed the deal.

We can map the broader sales process into these stages:

| Stage | Process Activity |
|---|---|
| Suspect | Customer Research; Needs Analysis |
| Prospect | Validation |
| Opportunity | Proposal; Presentation |
| Sale | Negotiation; Closing |

Table 1: Building a Sales Process

In Stage 1, we generate ideas of where there may be an opportunity; this requires us to research our customers and identify potential needs.

In Stage 2, we go to talk to the customer and confirm that there is a valid opportunity.

In Stage 3, we make a proposal / give a presentation of how we can satisfy the needs of the customer.

In Stage 4, we negotiate if required and close the deal.

This is about as simple a sales process as you can have. I recommend that as you identify activities, you categorise each of them into one of the four stages. In this way, you will be able to keep track of activity and balance activity between all four stages. A template for this is included in the exercises at the end of the book.

It is worthwhile trying to define metrics that can be used to track progress and define the progression of an opportunity from one stage to the next. These are likely to be related to the definition of a good opportunity, Chapter 17.

When trying to develop and refine these activities, try to include as many other sales people as possible to get a wide view of possible activities. Consider won and lost opportunities to know what worked and what did not work. You might even consider asking friendly customers to comment on what works for them and what does not.

Finally, your process should not be fixed in stone. It should evolve over time as you learn new techniques or have new ideas. At the conclusion of every deal, whether won or lost, review all of the activities and consider what was useful and what was not useful. Continue to refine your process as you go along.

# 4

## SELLING THROUGHOUT THE SALES PROCESS

*"The court generally moves in small steps rather than in one giant step."*

Ruth Bader Ginsburg

The sale of a product to every customer is made up of a number of smaller sales along the way. You will need to make an initial approach, have a number of meetings, make a presentation and negotiate before you ever shake hands on a deal. It might look something like the process below.

Figure 4.1        Opportunity Flow

At every stage in this process, you need to sell the next step. You are highly unlikely to make a sale at the end of a cold call. You will need to persuade the customer to meet with you, possibly meet again etc before you reach the end. It is a series of small steps. In every step, you have to think about what you want to achieve from that encounter, another meeting, meeting someone else, a presentation etc. Whatever it is, you need to know what you want in order to ask for it. It also pays to have a fallback position, something to agree as the next step if you fail to achieve your primary objective.

As you progress from point product sales to enterprise wide agreements, the length and complexity of this process will increase. It can take 1-2 years for some agreements to close and mapping out your process and working through it will be essential if you are to be successful. Gaining small commitments throughout will help you to feel successful and your customer to know that they are gaining something.

> Keep asking "Why does my customer care?"

Throughout, you must be continually asking yourself, "Why should my customer care about this?" or "Why should they be happy to move to the next stage?" You will both be aware of the end goal and its potential, but the customer has to know why each stage of the process is important and what they will get out of it. Everything you do should be to help to move the customer forwards and they should understand the value in moving forwards.

To be able to sell every stage, you may have to employ a number of tactics to help to persuade your customer that this is the right thing to do. There is a great video on YouTube called "Secrets from the Science of Persuasion" by Robert Cialdini and Steve Martin *https://www.youtube.com/watch?v=cFdCzN7RYbw.*

In the video, they talk about six ideas that can help you to persuade others to do what you would like them to do. Given that sales is all about persuading people to buy your product, these ideas are well worth reviewing. They are:

1. Reciprocity – Give before you receive;
2. Scarcity - People want more of those things that they can have less of;
3. Authority - People follow the lead of creditable, knowledgeable experts;
4. Consistency - Looking for commitments that can be made;
5. Liking - People who are similar to us;
6. Consensus – Doing what others are doing.

Let us look at each of these individually.

## Reciprocity

Reciprocity is about giving someone something in return for them doing something for you. If someone invites you to their house for dinner, it is usual to take them a gift. We are thanking them for inviting us and for the food that they are going to give us. Our gift is not equal in value to the dinner that they have prepared but we are acknowledging the effort and cost involved in feeding us.

Imagine that during this dinner, your hosts ask you to do them a favour. We feel more inclined to say yes, indeed we may feel obligated to say yes, because we are sitting in their house, eating their food. People are more likely to say yes to those that they owe. So, if you are the first to give, then the person that you give something to will be more likely to say yes if you then ask them to do something.

In a sales situation, this is an extremely useful tactic. Of course, the days of endless corporate hospitality in order to win work are no longer considered to be acceptable, precisely because they were designed to make the guests feel obliged to give the hosts an order. However, there are still ways in which you can give before you ask for something in return.

> If you give something to someone, they feel obligated to give you something in return.

For example, you can organise an event designed to showcase your product and include guest speakers that are not necessarily associated with your company and who talk about a general, relevant industry topic. Customers are more likely to come to this event than they are to accept a specific request to provide a product demonstration in their own offices. However, once they have attended, they are then more likely to host you in their offices, where you can start to develop them as a customer.

You can provide general, relevant, industry news or insight that your customer may not normally receive. If you do this without immediately asking for something in return, then when you are ready, ask for what you would like and the chances are, the customer will say yes. If a particular customer is proving difficult to get access to, consider sending them a gift. Ensure that what you give is appropriate to the person (as much as you can) and unexpected. That way, when you next contact them, they are again more likely to say yes.

**Scarcity**

People want more of those things that they can have less of. Any time there is a perception that a product might be in short supply, people tend to immediately stock up on that product. If a particular theatre show is running for a limited time only, demand for tickets is higher than for a show that is going to run for longer. Tickets for one-off events command higher prices than events that run regularly.

> People want more of those things that they can have less of.

If you have particular product that is scarce, or a resource that is particularly sought after, then you could have an advantage over your customer and can charge a premium for this. Alternatively, you can create a scarcity by limiting how much product you make or how much time you make your products available.

However, this is often difficult to preserve as your competition will start to copy you, or provide an 80% solution, which many customers will consider to be acceptable. What is more interesting and useful to consider is, what might a customer stand to lose by not using your product and what is unique about your product.

What might a customer lose by not adopting your products? This has become popularised recently with the expression "fear of missing out" or FOMO. In popular culture, this manifests itself as not being at certain events or not having the latest app or gadget. However, in business, it can be just as relevant. If lots of companies are adopting a technology, then the ones who are not adopting it are missing out and this is something to make them aware of. What does everyone else know that they do not know? It may not be that critical but it is a way of creating an opportunity for you.

It is critically important to know what is unique about your product. What is it that you do or offer that no one else can offer? This is essentially why your customer will choose your product. If you can determine what it is that drives a customer to need this particular feature, then you can identify these potential customers for your product and work on selling to them. We will discuss this in more detail in Chapter 16, Why are you Unique?

**Authority**

We inherently follow orders from policemen and firemen in a time of crisis. We believe that they are more knowledgeable about a situation and its impact on us and therefore we do as we are told. We respect their authority. There is an expression in business that you must have a few grey hairs before you will be taken seriously. This just means that with age comes experience and that people respect experience. So, people will follow the lead of creditable, knowledgeable experts and believe that the advice that they offer will be sensible and worthwhile. There are two ways that you can use this to your advantage.

Who can you get to introduce you to a customer? We implicitly trust people who are trusted by other people that we trust. This is why business networking is effective and websites like LinkedIn are so popular. They all allow us to get introduced to people who can introduce us to others. So, if you want to get an introduction to a customer, try to find someone that you know in common and get them to introduce you. This is particularly effective within a single company, particularly if your contact can introduce you in person. Always take the opportunity to be introduced to others if you are given it. You never know when a contact may become useful.

> People follow the lead of creditable, knowledgeable experts.

In addition, is there a way that you can get referrals from your existing customers? Can you persuade them to tell others who might want your product? If you can build this into your standard way of working, then you can effectively use your customers as your business development team. People who have received great service will tell others about it and will tell people enthusiastically which will make others want to use your service even more.

How can you position yourselves as credible experts? At the very least, you are an expert in your own business and product. However, can you build an image of yourself that makes everyone believe that you are an expert in your field? Can you recruit someone who already has this respect? If so, you are likely to gain credibility and people will want to do business with you. Use your own qualifications whenever they are relevant. Write articles and technical papers as often as possible. The more that you can get yourself in print, the more you will be seen as an expert. You do not have to present your product. Indeed, I suggest that you do not present it. If you impress people with your expertise, they will seek you out to buy your product.

## Consistency

In essence, people are more likely to say yes to people that they have said yes to in the past. So, when you are trying to sell something to a customer, asking them to buy in the first meeting is unlikely to receive a positive response. However, if you continually ask for small commitments, then by the time that you ask them for a signature on an agreement, they are used to saying yes.

Imagine that you went to buy a pair of shoes. You are likely to find a pair that you like in the shop and ask the assistant if they have that pair in your size. Suppose that the assistant found that pair, brought them to you and immediately asked if you wanted to buy them. I guess that this would not elicit a great reaction and you might be inclined to not buy them. Instead, they will ask if you want to try them on, then would you like to walk around the shop in them. They would then ask if they are comfortable, do they fit well, do they rub your feet in any part, do you like the look of them? Only once they have asked all of these questions, do they ask if you want to buy the shoes.

Fortunately, sales is a process and we have to move though each step of the sales process to get to the end. As a result, we are constantly asking our customer for small commitments along the way. Can we talk for a few minutes? Can we have a meeting? Can we meet with the other members of the team? Can we present the product to a wider audience? Every time you ask for the next step in the process, you get the customer to say yes.

> Ask your customer for a number of small commitments before ever asking them to buy your product.

All of this makes it much easier for them to say yes at the end. If it is a relatively simple sale, with few steps in the process, I suggest that you include a number of additional questions or steps along the way to get more positive responses. This is a bit like an indirect closing technique or the question close. In this, the salesperson moves to the close with a series of indirect or soft questions such as "How do you feel about these terms" or "how does this agreement look to you?" Again, you are looking for small commitments that lead to towards the final main commitment.

## Liking

Put very simply, we like people who are similar to us, who pay us compliments and who cooperate with us. We are much more likely to do business with people who we like than with people who we do not like. Of course, it is very difficult to force people to like us so we have to try to develop that liking over time. This is very similar to "Building Trust", which we will discuss in Chapter 5.

> We like people who are similar to us and we buy from people that we like.

To make people like us, we have to be interested in them and what they are doing. When you meet with a customer, try to get to know them as a person before you ever talk business. This does not mean that you do not talk business for the whole of a meeting, but spend some time at the start getting to know each other. Tell them about your background, what brought you to where you are today. Try to get them to do the same. Be interested in what they have to say and ask questions. Be complimentary as much as possible. If we are told that we have done a great thing, then we feel good about ourselves and we like the person that has told us that. Do not rush them when they are telling a story, no matter how much you want to get down to business. If the customer is happy to talk, then let them talk. It is quite possible that they will tell you important information as part of their commentary which you can use later in the process.

Of course, it may not be possible to get everyone to like us. There will be times when, for whatever reason, we do not see eye to eye with a customer. In this instance, it is probably better to ask someone else to deal with them rather than trying to get them to like you. The effort that it will take to get them to change their mind is not worth it when someone else can take over. I was once standing in for a colleague who was on maternity leave. I was managing a particular customer and was struggling to build a relationship with the person in procurement who we were having to deal with. To this day I do not know why it was difficult. I had actually never met him; all of our conversations had been over the phone, which may not have helped. However, I just could not get on with them and it was spoiling the relationship between our companies. As soon as my colleague came back, I was delighted to hand over responsibility for this customer. She called him and within 10 minutes she knew most of his life history, the names of his dogs and was well on the way to establishing a good relationship with him.

It is important not take business personally. While we all want to be liked, do not let your effort to be liked get in the way of being successful. Doing the right thing for the customer sometimes means stepping away, no matter what the potential prize on offer.

## Consensus

We all have a tendency to want to jump on the bandwagon, follow the herd or keep up with the Joneses. Humans like to be with other humans and get involved with what others are doing. If you have customers who are all adopting a particular process or technology, for example, let other customers know. They will probably want to get involved, particularly if they are similar companies. If they see that other companies are gaining an advantage over them, or even perceive that they are gaining an advantage, then they will want to be involved. Highlighting the success of one customer is a great way of attracting new ones.

> People will follow what others are doing and buy what others are buying.

Case histories and success stories, particularly told from the perspective of the customer rather than the supplier, are a great way of creating consensus. They highlight the success that someone has had by deploying a new process and essentially create jealousy. We want to be successful like others. The more ways that you can highlight the success that a customer has had from using your product, the more you create consensus and persuade other to follow. We discuss Case Histories in more detail in Chapter 15, Why Change?

**How to ask for a decision**

You should always think about how you phrase your request to a customer. Logically, our decision to say "yes" would consider a careful analysis of pros and cons and be informed by existing preferences. We would always make optimal decisions. However, our decisions to buy are quite often influenced by how the offer is presented to us. There are ways that are more likely to get a positive response than others.

Consider this scenario:

Would you rather

 1.   Have a certain win of £10,000, or
 2.   A 25% chance to win £40,000 and a 75% chance to win nothing?

In this scenario, most people will choose Option 1, the certain win – we would rather gain something than nothing. If we now reverse the scenario:

Would you rather

 1.   Have a certain loss of £30,000, or
 2.   A 75% chance to lose £40,000 and a 25% chance to lose nothing?

In this scenario, more people will choose Option 2, where they stand a chance to lose nothing. The odds on losing nothing are 1 in 4 as are the odds of winning £40,000 in the first scenario but more people will choose those odds, simply because of the way that the offer is presented.

This happens because we dislike losses more than we like an equivalent gain. Giving something up is more painful than the pleasure we derive from receiving it. This is a subtle change but can greatly influence how an offer is received. As a result, the more that you can eliminate the possibility of a loss and the more that you can increase the probability of a gain, the more successful your offer will be.

**Behavioural Economics**

Behavioural economics is the study of psychology behind the decision-making that leads to an economic outcome, such as the factors influencing a consumer buying one product instead of another. The US academic Richard Thaler won the Nobel prize in economics for his pioneering work in this field.

Unlike the field of classical economics, in which decision-making is entirely based on cold-headed logic, behavioural economics allows for irrational behaviour and attempts to understand why this may be the case. The concept can be applied in miniature to individual situations, or more broadly to encompass the wider actions of a society or trends in financial markets. It was used extensively in decisions relating to the Covid-19 pandemic to persuade people to live safely.

Thaler is particularly well known for his work on "nudge theory", a term he coined to help explain how small interventions can encourage individuals to make different decisions. Nudge theory suggests changes can be made to an individual's "choice environment" to influence their behaviour. The best example of this comes in the supermarket, where attention can be drawn to certain products to encourage consumers to spend money. It also resulted in a change in the way organ donation was managed. Originally, people were asked to opt in to organ donation resulting in a certain take up. However, when the process was changed such that individuals had to opt out of donation, fewer people opted out resulting in a larger number of potential organ donors.

When you are communicating with your customer, try to think about your words. Can you try to persuade a customer to think that what you want them to do is actually their own idea? If you can do this, then you have a greater chance of success. Think about how you position your offer. Can you create a bundle that increases the value of the deal to you without it being too obvious to the customer? How can you nudge the customer along into making a decision to change and to use your product? Can you send them information that relates to how others have been successful by using the product?

**Keeping them warm**

Once you have met a potential customer, you must stay in contact with them. Your products may be of value to them in the future and the last thing that you want is to have to go about introducing yourself to them all over again. You have to keep them as a warm customer rather than a cold customer. There are a number of ways that you can go about this.

Social media is here to stay, whether we like it or not. While it started out as a way to stay in touch with friends, it has become so much more than that. The majority of advertising money is now spent on social media so it is something that you have to engage with, whether you like it or not. This book is all about selling so I do not propose to discuss marketing via social media here. There are many more books about social media marketing that are written by much more knowledgeable people than me. However, it is important that you include some element of social media in your work.

For business to business sales people, the main tool for this is LinkedIn. You should try to engage with your customers regularly on LinkedIn. This way, you can quickly and easily keep in touch without directly contacting them. You can like or share their posts. Better still, comment on them. By being the first to do this, you will encourage your customer to do the same for you, which increases your reach as well as building trust with your customer.

Make sure that you post information on the site on a regular basis. This way, your potential customers will "see" you regularly. The information does not have to be about your own products, it could be generally useful information. Reposting other people's useful information is also worthwhile. In part, it saves you having to think of anything new to post! It also demonstrates your value to customers and suggests that you are worth doing business with.

Social media is essentially a one-way form of communication. You push information out and you hope that the customer sees it. Only if they interact with it can you be sure that they have seen it. It is therefore important to have more direct contact with customers in a non-sales way. Sending useful information every so often is a great way to do this. You are not asking for anything in return - remember reciprocity? You are simply providing useful information, gently reminding the customer about your products and helping to educate them.

> Stay in touch with all of your customers on a regular basis; if you do, then they will be easier to sell to.

Other ways to stay in touch should also be used whenever possible. Arrange to see them at an exhibition or conference where you are attending or presenting. Call them up when you are passing their office and see if they have time for a coffee. It is quite likely that they will not be available but they will appreciate the offer. However, if they do accept, then you know that they are still interested to do business with you. In this case, I suggest that you do not talk about your products. Let them do all of the talking. You will learn a lot that you can use later in the sales process and you will earn their gratitude.

However you go about doing it, you must stay in touch with potential customers and keep them warm. Research suggests that it takes between 6 and 9 contacts with a customer before they are ready to buy. Most sales people give up after 2 or 3. Apply all of the science of persuasion to your interactions with them and you will find them much more accepting of your products. Research has shown that nurtured leads increase the likelihood of a sale and make larger purchases than non-nurtured leads.

# Trust

Definition (from Oxford English Dictionary)

1.  (n) Firm belief in the reliability, truth, or ability of someone or something.
2.  (n) Reliance on the truth of a statement without examination.
3.  (v) Believe in, rely on the character or behaviour of.

# 5

## BUILDING TRUST

*"People don't care how much you know, until they know how much you care."*

Theodore Roosevelt

The first stage of The Equation of Sales is Trust. Fundamentally, no one buys from someone that they do not trust. At least, no one buys at the full price from someone that they do not trust. Most people will have met someone in a bar who has tried to sell them something cheap but the cheap price gives away that the seller is possibly not to be trusted. They are just trying to tempt you with a cheap price. At a car boot or garage sale, prices are cheap because the buyer has no come back against the seller, there is no trust.

In business, we have to trust the people that we do business with. Without that, we are unlikely to proceed. So, the first job for any sales person is to build that trust. With some roles, that trust is implicit. We trust a doctor when we go to see them. "Trust me, I'm a doctor" is said in a jokey way but comes from the fact that we do trust doctors. We know that they have spent at least 5 years training to be able to treat us and that means that we trust them to look after us.

> The first job for any sales person is to build trust.

Over the years, we have always trusted people in certain professions. We trust that the fire brigade will come to help us if we call them, even if it is only to rescue a cat in a tree. Trust comes with the role in these instances. However, a sales person who arrives on your door step has none of those advantages so the first thing that they have to do is to build trust.

The reason that so many people do not trust sales people is that they, quite reasonably in some cases, have a poor reputation. People who sold second hand cars many years ago were not always entirely honest. Double glazing sales people employed all sorts of ruses and tricks to persuade people to buy new windows on their first visit. Their behaviour was driven entirely by their desire to earn commission in the easiest possible way. Care for their customer was fairly low on the list of their priorities.

No sales person who wants to be taken seriously, to help their customer over a long time, can afford to be untrustworthy. However, that trust must to be earned; it does not come automatically.

> Trust has to be earned; it does not come automatically.

Businesses today invest a lot of time and effort in building their credibility and trustworthiness. Schemes like;

CheckaTrade (https://www.checkatrade.com/) or
TrustMark (https://www.trustmark.org.uk/)

are UK organisations that exist to help companies to demonstrate that they are trustworthy. Business networking groups exist to allow people to build trust with each other and to win recommendations. ISO certifications, British Standards etc are there for companies to provide reassurance that their services comply with agreed standards so that we can trust them.

However, companies are made up of people and it is the people we deal with that we really have to trust. It is they who come to see us, offer us their service and take our money. We must trust them as people, as much as we trust the company that they work for, before we will consider buying from them. Long established businesses will employ a variety of sales people and if they visit an existing customer, they are generally given an audience as their company is known and trusted. However, they still have to take some time to establish their own personal trust. Do not expect to make sales with a customer just because they have bought from your company in the past.

> We must trust sales people before we will consider buying from them.

To a large extent, if I like you, I am more likely to trust you. As a result, getting your potential customer to like you is the first stage of building trust. It is not essential to be liked but I do believe that it helps dramatically. Your customer may respect you and that may be sufficient to enable you to build trust but it will take longer. Of course, it is difficult to be liked if you do not like your customer and that can happen. These circumstances make it difficult to build a good relationship and, in these instances, it may be better to have someone else look after the relationship, if that is possible, or focus your efforts elsewhere.

Of course, sometimes it is not possible to hand over responsibility like this. If you are the only sales person or there is no alternative, you have to either make it work as well as possible or decide that the customer is not worth the effort.

> If I like you, I am more likely to trust you.

Many years ago, I got a card through the door from a company offering solar panels to reduce heating bills. This was before solar panels and solar farms became quite so common. I was interested to know more, so invited the company to come to see me. When their representative turned up, there was some basic trust as he came from a company that I was aware of. However, he was still required to build some trust with me personally. In an attempt to build some rapport, he asked me some basic questions. The conversation went something like this:

Him: "What do you do for a living?"

Me: "I sell computer software to help to find oil and gas."

Him: "That's a bit different but I guess that someone has to do it."

He lost the potential sale there and then. He was sitting in my house, in the evening, trying to sell me solar panels and he poured scorn on my job. Failing to show interest in my job, even faked interest, demonstrated that he really did not care about me.

By spending time advising customers, consistently delivering against expectations and delivering valuable solutions, you will become highly valued by your customer. You will become a trusted advisor. As a trusted advisor, your customer will come to you for advice on all sorts of things, not just on the products that you sell. If they do need what you offer, then their buying process will be shorter and less complicated and they will buy more and more from you.

Not being a trusted advisor does not prevent you from selling. Indeed, you will have to make a number of sales that prove to be of value and as promised in order to demonstrate that you can be fully trusted. Your first sales to a company may be difficult while you build your reputation. However, once you have proven yourself, they will get easier and easier.

Trust is built one interaction and one sale at a time. You cannot just decide to be a trusted advisor because you would like to be. So, building trust, selling relevant solutions, delivering against expectations are all things that you must do along the way to becoming a trusted advisor.

**First impressions count!**

The best opportunity that you have for building trust is the first few minutes that you meet someone. You may have spoken to them on the phone to set up the appointment, so you will have formed some impression on your customer. However, the biggest impact you will have is in the first few minutes that you meet them in the flesh.

Harvard Business School professor, Amy Cuddy, has been studying first impressions alongside fellow psychologists Susan Fiske and Peter Glick for more than 15 years, and has discovered patterns in these interactions. Her book, called "Presence", discusses how first impressions influence our perception of people. In summary, people quickly answer two questions when they first meet you:

- Can I trust this person?
- Can I respect this person?

Psychologists refer to these dimensions as warmth and competence, respectively, and ideally you want to be perceived as having both.

Interestingly, Cuddy says that most people, especially in a professional context, believe that competence is the more important factor. After all, they want to prove that they are smart and talented enough to handle your business.

But in fact, warmth, or trustworthiness, is the most important factor in how people evaluate you. A warm, trustworthy person, who is also strong, elicits admiration, but only after you have established trust does your strength become a gift rather than a threat.

> Warmth, or trustworthiness, is the most important factor in how people evaluate you when they first meet you.

"From an evolutionary perspective," Cuddy says, "it is more crucial to our survival to know whether a person deserves our trust." It makes sense when you consider that in cavemen days it was more important to figure out if your fellow man was going to kill you and steal all your possessions than if he was competent enough to build a good fire.

## What is important on first impressions?

There are some basic things that I believe you must do in order to immediately make a good impression.

**Turn up on time.** This is a pretty basic thing and one of the most important. Turning up late does not make a good impression. Even if your customer is late, you cannot be. If you have a tendency to be late, make sure that you leave earlier than normal. Plan your travel time as well as your meeting time. While it may be acceptable to occasionally be late once you have built a relationship, if you are late on your first appointment, that does not demonstrate reliability. If you find that, through no fault of your own, you are going to be late, make sure that you let your customer know. Text or email them once it is clear that you are going to be late and explain the reason for your delay. Once you arrive, apologise and try to ensure that it never happens again.

**Be presentable.** This does not necessarily mean wear your best outfit. It means dress appropriately for the customer that you are going to see. My general rule is to wear something slightly smarter than your customer. If you wear something too smart, you may appear pompous and stuffy; if you wear something too casual, you risk being considered trivial or worse, disrespectful. So, if your customer typically wears jeans and a tee shirt, smart trousers / skirt and shirt / blouse are fine. If they wear a suit, you should wear a suit. You do not have to go over the top with your suit. While a morning / evening suit is one up from a lounge suit, it is probably not appropriate for a business meeting!

**Be polite.** This is pretty obvious and should go without saying. Say please and thank you; if you are offered a drink, accept one, even if it is only a glass of water. If you have a number of meetings in a day, constantly drinking coffee may not be the best thing to do but there is nothing wrong with accepting water. Accept that your customer may be a bit rushed and late, try to relax and accept the situation rather than getting annoyed

**Be friendly.** Smile and greet your customer with a good handshake. Speak clearly and make eye contact. Asking interesting questions, unrelated to work to demonstrate an interest in your customer as a person. Just because you are there to talk business, does not mean that you cannot take an interest in them. If you rush into talking about business, you miss your best opportunity to build rapport with your customer. There will be plenty of time to talk business but you cannot go back and talk about the weather, football or the upcoming holidays once you are in your meeting.

> Find out about your customer in advance so that you have something to talk when you meet them.

To ensure that these initial minutes are successful, it helps to plan for them in advance. Try to find out what your customer looks like so that you know when they are coming to meet you. Stand up and go to greet them. Prepare something relevant to say. Not, "do you come here often" but maybe comment on the artwork in the lobby or refer to someone that you both know. Small talk does not come easily to everyone so to be successful at it, you must think about it in advance.

There is a classic scene in the film, Bridget Jones' Diary where, at an important event, Bridget is recommended to introduce people by sharing interesting information about them. You can watch it here.

*https://www.youtube.com/watch?v=5F53uo5hxFQ*

While you might not want to go that far, you might consider sharing useful or relevant information with your customer while you are getting set for the meeting. You should know if they have made any important announcements recently. If they have been successful, offer congratulations. Try to demonstrate, not only that you are aware of what they do but that you want to help them to be successful by providing some insight that they may not be aware of.

Engaging with insights is a great way to start an engagement. Sharing interesting, relevant content demonstrates not only that you have taken time to know about their business but that you are there to support them. This is even more beneficial if you have nothing to gain from providing the insight. We are more likely to trust people who pass on knowledge without seeking to gain from it.

Rachel Botsman, the author of "Who Can You Trust?" and a fellow at Oxford Business School, states that there are four traits of trustworthiness: competence, reliability, empathy and integrity.

**Competence.** This is the ability of a person to do a specific task. It will vary from task to task. I am competent at teaching sales skills but I am not competent at taking a penalty to win a world cup final! If you want someone to trust you, you have to demonstrate that you are competent at the task that they will want you to do.

**Reliability.** This refers to a person's consistency to do what they said they would do on numerous occasions. Ultimately, it is about knowing that you can depend on this person in the long term.

**Empathy.** This is the capacity to understand or feel what another person is experiencing from within their frame of reference. This means feeling sad when they are sad or happy when they are happy. This requires you to be sincere and open, to care for the person you are talking to.

**Integrity.** This is about intentions and motives. We want to believe that someone wants the same as ourselves. This is critical in sales – we want to focus on making our clients successful rather than making ourselves successful. If they are successful then we will be but the focus has to be on them.

> Competence, reliability, empathy and integrity are the four traits of trustworthiness.

## Telling Stories

If you consider our best relationships, they all involve telling stories. Our children tell us what they have done that day, our friends recount their adventures when we are on a night out, we get to know our partners by telling stories of our life.

We remember stories much more than we remember facts. Our brains treat stories differently from other kinds of information. Stories tend to arouse emotions in each of us which we can relate to much better than facts. As a result, we understand them better, remember them more accurately, and we find them more engaging to listen to in the first place.

Stories also avoid pushback because it is very hard to argue with a story. Your customer cannot dispute your life story, the reason your company was created, etc. If you lead with facts, people may try to dispute them or doubt them if they have no reference.

> Stories are one of the best ways of communicating and they are a great way to build a relationship.

I highly recommend reading this book, "Seven Stories every Salesperson Must Tell", by Mike Adams. Mike goes into a lot of detail about how to build a story and the different types of story that are useful in the sales process. These include:

- Hook stories – to connect you to the customer
- Insight stories – to differentiate you from the competition
- Landing stories – to help you to close the deal.

Hook stories, such as your personal story, the story behind your company etc are used when you first meet a new customer. They are used for introduction and to build rapport. Mike suggests that once you have told your personal story, you should invite your customer to share theirs. This way, you build a bond based on your stories.

Of course, you must make your story interesting and reasonably relevant. All good stories have a complication along the way, something that creates suspense or drama. Without a twist, we are just recounting a sequence of events. So, think about the various events in your life that have led you to where you are now. Think about the twists and turns and the life changing events that have happened. Build your story out of these events. We discuss this more in the next Chapter, Why do you do what you do?

## Cultural Differences

For anyone who works across different countries, it is important to bear in mind that different countries work in different ways and the people in those countries behave in a different way. Most people will know that there are differences between Americans, Australians, Japanese and French people. However, there are subtleties of differences between some countries that must be appreciated in order to be successful. In order to build trust with someone from another country, it is important to understand the differences between your country and theirs.

Professor Geert Hofstede conducted one of the most comprehensive studies of how values in the workplace are influenced by culture. He defines culture as "the collective programming of the mind distinguishing the members of one group or category of people from others". This gave rise to the six dimensions of national culture which are used worldwide in both academic and professional management settings. Many more details can be found here, *www.geerthofstede.com*.

If you are working with people of different nationalities, I strongly recommend that you review the information here. I was recently working with a British person who worked for an Italian company trying to sell a product to a Malaysian company. Understanding the cultural differences between all of them was crucial to success!

## Strategies for Building Trust

Once we have established some relationship with our customer, we have to build on it and demonstrate why they should continue to trust us.

> Building trust is not a one-off activity; it continues throughout our relationship with our customers.

To this end, there are some important elements to continuing to build trust. These are things that should become automatic in all of your engagements with a customer. Your behaviour must continually reinforce the view that you can be trusted.

**Say what you are going to do and then do what you say!** At the end of any meeting with a customer, agree to some actions going forwards. This may be to provide answers to some questions, provide pricing details or clarify an offer. Agree what you will do for the customer, and potentially what they will do for you, and a time frame for completion. Then, ensure that you deliver on your promises before the completion date. If, for any reason, you are unable to do this, ensure that you inform the customer.

**Communicate, communicate, communicate.** This follows from the last point but maintaining communication with your potential customer is very important. We will discuss this in a number of chapters but staying in regular contact, even when there is no sale imminent, will help you in the longer term.

**Appreciate long term relationships more than short term success.** It is tempting to try to close deals quickly and move on to the next one. However, you run the risk of being seen as transactional and not interested in the customer. Short term deals will keep you going for a short time, well-built relationships will keep you going for the rest of your working life. So, focus more on your core principles and customer loyalty than short term commissions and profits.

**Be honest!** There is never a good reason to be dishonest with your customer. If your product cannot do something, let them know. It may just be a nice to have rather than a critical issue for them so it may not be a deal breaker. However, if it is critical and you tell them that you can do it when you cannot, then you are creating lots of problems for yourself. If a product is going to be late, let the customer know. If a project is going to be late or worst still, fail, let the customer know. They would rather know early, when they may be able to do something about it, than too late when they cannot.

**Always do the right thing.** Most people know what the right thing to do is in most situations. A former manager of mine used to say, if you are prepared to accept reading about what you have done in the newspaper the next day, then you are probably OK. If not, then you are probably not doing the right thing. When you do not do the right thing, admit it. Be transparent, authentic and willing to share your mistakes and faults.

These general activities are mostly reactive, in that they happen because of an interaction with your customer. It is important to also be proactive by doing things for your customer without being asked.

**Tactics for Building Trust**

In general, this involves doing small, unrequested activities to help your customer. What you want to do is to coach your customers. Help them to be better and to learn more. Do not keep information to yourself that might be of benefit to your customer. The more information you provide to your customer, the more that they will trust you. It can be quite straight forward to provide information that you have that is not confidential but can benefit the customer. When you do this when there is no sale involved, you become trusted even quicker. You are showing that you care about them as a person rather than as just a customer.

This could be information about your product but that is a rather narrow range of information. Much better to share information that you have that they might be interested in but may not have seen. Industry information, hints and tips, even information about their favourite team or band! It does not have to be about what you are selling. The purpose is to build trust and selflessly providing information is a great way to do this.

I recommend that you define a series of actions that you can take on a regular basis to help you to build trust with your customers. Some may be relevant only when you meet with them, others may be done remotely. Regularly think about how you might improve these activities or add to them over time. Try not to repeat the same things for each customer unless they are things that are reasonable to repeat, such as an annual user group meeting or similar. Doing these things will help you to proactively build trust with your customer.

There are examples of this with the exercises at the end of the book.

# 6

## WHY DO YOU DO WHAT YOU DO?

*"Approach each customer with the idea of helping him or her solve a problem or achieve a goal, not of selling a solution or service."*

Brian Tracy

There is a great TED talk by Simon Sinek which discusses how great leaders inspire action. You can watch it here:

*https://www.ted.com/talks/simon_sinek_how_great_leaders_inspire_action.*

I urge you to watch it before reading this chapter. Indeed, I recommend that you watch it a few times as I will readily admit that I needed to watch it a few times before I appreciated all of it.

The premise of the talk is that people follow great leaders because of why they are doing something not because of what they are doing. He urges you to think about your "why" – why do you do what you do? This is obviously important for anyone in any job but is even more important in sales. Belief in your own product is critical to being successful. Customers will be able to see through any sales person who does not think that their product can help the customer. You do not necessarily have to have bought one yourself but you have to believe that it will give value to the customer.

> People will believe in you because of why you do things, not what you do.

Simon Sinek states that why you do something is not for the end result. Businesses make a profit but that is not why they exist. They exist because a small number of people thought that they could make a difference. They were inspired to do something different.

Apple Computers was founded in April 1976, by Steve Jobs and Steve Wozniak. They both dropped out of college with a vision of changing the way people viewed computers. Jobs and Wozniak wanted to make computers small enough for people to have in their homes or offices. They wanted to build user friendly computers that were accessible to everyone. Apple not only changed the way that we view computers but also the way that we now consume music, videos and make phone calls. They focussed on challenging the status quo and made beautiful products.

Likewise, Google, Facebook, eBay etc. all started with the desire to change things, to create something new. I suspect that the desire to be rich and famous was not uppermost in the minds of the people who started those companies. It took a lot of time and effort to make them successful. Their founders persevered despite the many hurdles in their way because they believed in what they were doing not because they thought that they might get rich.

The people that joined these companies afterwards were clearly not as driven as the founders to create change but they still believed in the company, in their ethos and what they were trying to achieve. If they did not, then their motivation to get out of bed in the morning was going to be sadly lacking.

People selling on behalf of companies must believe in the motivation of that company and the products that they create. Human beings are emotional creatures and emotion lies behind most of our decisions. You might think that logic lies behind most buying decisions but actually, it is the opposite.

> People buy based on emotion and justify their decision with logic and reason.

As a result, we have to appeal to their emotions before we engage logically. To do this successfully, we must be emotionally engaged by the company and product that we are selling. This requires an understanding of the history of the company and the product that you are selling. Talking about the blood, sweat and tears that went into its creation engages emotionally and also explains to the potential buyer why the company was founded.

Most companies are founded to exploit an opportunity, whether that is the exclusive right to explore for oil, new technology to develop personal computers or a way of connecting people across the internet. If you are trying to sell this to another company, they are quite likely to be suffering from similar problems so sharing the history of the company will strike a chord with them.

As discussed in the previous chapter, our minds treat stories differently from other kinds of information. We understand them better, remember them more accurately and we find them more engaging to listen to in the first place.

The company creation story is a Hook Story according to "Seven Stories every Salesperson Must Tell", by Mike Adams. It allows the customer to understand the background and reasons for its existence, the struggle that it went through to become successful and the products that it offers. This helps to build trust with the potential customer and explains the company's "why" – why does it exist? Why does it do what it does?

All of this has to be explained in a fairly short time without too much detail to avoid your audience switching off. The critical part of the story is the turning point. Businesses tend to struggle to begin with so what made this one successful? This is where the real emotion of the story is and will hook your audience.

It is difficult for people who are not the founders of a company to tell these stories with the same passion and emotional resonance as the founders. Also, for companies that were founded many years ago, the story has some less resonance. However, there it is likely that the product that you are selling is relatively new and you can apply the same theory to the story behind a product as you can to the story behind your company.

**Your Story**

The one story that you should be an expert in is your story. This introduces you to a customer in a relevant and meaningful way that explains how you come to be in the position that you are. There are many different editions of this story and you will need to pick the right one for each customer. To help, think about it this way.

**When did you start this role?** It is important to anchor your story in time so that the customer can also place themselves at this time. There is a big difference between having started last month and having started ten years ago. All good stories have to be given a time reference.

**What were you doing before this role?** We all have some past. What was your last role, whether this was university / college or a completely different job? What was the trigger for ending that? Why did you leave? You may have had a short-term contract; you may have come to the end of your college course; you may have been made redundant; you may have not liked your boss and left. There is no shame in any of these. There is always a reason for a role coming to an end and it brought you to where you are now.

**What made you want to do this current role?** When you were looking for a new position, what was it about this specific company or role that attracted you? It may have been the person you were working for; it may have been the freedom to be creative; it may have been the products that you get to work with. Something made you take this role, what was it?

> You should be able to easily explain to a customer why you do what you do.

**What inspires you?** Everyone is motivated by something or someone at their work. What is it for you? What have you learnt since you started working here that makes you want to continue to work here?

**What is it about the product that you sell that that excites you?** Something about it has to be exciting otherwise you will never raise the energy to talk about it to anyone. What makes you think "this is really cool" or "I wish I had one of those".

**Why are you different?** What makes you different from everyone else out there? Is it your character? Your ambition? Your desire to help others? Something makes you stand out from the crowd and this should be obvious to your customer.

From all of this, you should have enough information to be able to write down "**Why you do what you do**?"

If I was to answer these questions, I might say the following;

*"I worked for a service company in the oil industry. About 5 years ago, due to a down turn in the industry associated with a low oil price, my role was made redundant and rather than find a new job, I chose to start my own consultancy. I had always thought that I would do this at some point in my career although I had not quite anticipated it quite this early. It was about this time that my wife and I were looking to buy a new house and we met with a number of estate agents who really did not do a great job. It made me realise that lots of people in sales roles have probably not been trained, or trained well, to sell effectively. I knew that I could help them to do their job better so I decided to take the plunge and work for myself. I had absolutely nothing to work with when I started, everything that I use in my training I have created myself. Nothing that has happened since has persuaded me that I was wrong; I see examples of poor sales almost every day. I'm determined that we can do this better."*

It is very important, not only for your own peace of mind, but for your sales pitch, to be excited by the products that you sell. That passion will be transmitted to your customers and they will get excited by your excitement. Knowing why you are where you are, why your company was formed and why you do what you do, all feed that passion.

Having read all of this, I suggest that you go back and re-watch the video,

*https://www.ted.com/talks/simon_sinek_how_great_leaders_inspire_ac tion.*

# 7

## CUSTOMER RESEARCH

*"If you steal from one author it is plagiarism; if you steal from many, its research."*

Wilson Mizner

You might wonder why customer research is part of trust. It is the first stage of the sales process and comes before we have even met with our potential customer. Think about it this way, imagine going to see a potential customer and having no idea about their business. How awkward is that conversation going to be?

If your customer is going to trust you, you must be credible. This means that you have to know something about them before you ever go to see them. You have to at least know that they might want to buy your product. Better still, you should be reasonably confident that you can discover a good reason for them to want to buy it. If you do not think this in advance, then you are probably wasting everyone's time.

> Before you ever go to see a customer, you should have a good idea that they might need your product.

If you sell shoes, you can reasonably assume that, sooner or later, most people will want to buy a pair. Therefore, a sensible thing to do is to open a shop and wait for people to come to you. However, if yours is the fifth shoe shop to open on a small high street, then you might not get the footfall you require to be profitable. Much better to open up on a high street with no competition. This is a reasonable approach for goods that everyone needs. However, for more specialised goods, you cannot expect your customer to just come to you, so you must proactively seek your potential customers.

To be successful when proactively seeking new customers, you have to narrow down the number of customers you try to talk to. This is relatively easy if your product is only really used in a specific vertical market, less so for products that work across all industries

For example, the technology that a scientist might use in the oil industry is probably only used by oil companies and some service companies within the oil industry. As a result, it is relatively easy to define the potential customers – anyone who employs that type of scientist. However, not all scientists will necessarily need the product and there are several hundred oil companies in Europe alone. Some prioritisation of these is still required.

For a technology that works across all industries, it is likely that sales people will be assigned to one or more vertical markets. So, one sales person for a document management system may be assigned to the energy industry, another to the defence industry and another to the finance industry. Many of the companies in each vertical market will have similar needs associated with their particular industry so there are reasonable synergies to be found. Equally, many of these companies will have similar departments such as HR, accounting or IT. They are potentially going to have the same needs regardless of which industry they serve. Focussing sales at these functional groups is another way of organising your effort.

However you are organised and whichever companies you are targeting, you must know something about them before you ever go to meet with them. It is often said that sales people are lucky because they turned up just at the time that the customer needed their product. Without any research, they may get lucky a couple of times but that will not last. To turn up at the right time all of the time, you must have done your research correctly.

> If you have done your research correctly, you should be meeting your customer just before they need your product.

I recently received an email that read like this (I have changed the words slightly to avoid it being obvious who might have sent it).

*Hello Tim,*

*I am emailing you about the possibility of meeting for an informal chat to discuss your future plans for Hoolock Consulting Limited.*

*Our Research team has identified your business as one of the most saleable in your market place so I would like to speak with you about your plans.*

*If you'd like to talk about this over a coffee then just let me know your availability and I will make the necessary arrangements.*

*I look forward to hearing from you.*

*Kind regards,*

*A Salesman*

There are two major problems with this email. Firstly, Hoolock Consulting employs one person and has no tangible assets. I cannot see how this makes it a great opportunity for anyone who is looking to buy another company. Secondly, the email came from a person based 200 miles from my office so it was going to be a long way to come for a coffee to discuss no opportunity. Suffice to say, I was not terribly impressed with their research and did not take them up on the offer.

To avoid looking like a fool, and thereby ensuring that you are never invited to a meeting ever again, it is important to have an idea of why a particular company might want your products. This is particularly important if you have no relationship with them. If you want to be successful with them, you are going to have to get in touch with them and persuade them to meet with you. This means that you have to tempt them with what your product can do for them and that will be difficult if you do not know anything about them. We will discuss how to tempt them in Chapter 9, How to get through the front door.

Potential customers generally fall into one of two categories. Those that we have a good idea that they will want our product and those that we just have a general idea that they may want our product. We generally require some specific evidence that gives us our good idea. For all the others, we have to know as much about them as possible so that we can have a sensible conversation with them once we have got through the front door.

### Where do good ideas come from?

If you Google "where do good ideas come from", the first twenty or so links are all about the same thing. It is a book written by Steven Johnson called "Where Good Ideas Come From: The Seven Patterns of Innovation". In the book, he identifies key principles that are the driving force of creativity. The simple premise is that there is very little that is totally new. Most new ideas come from rearranging and reconnecting different pieces of information. It is also discussed in this YouTube video,

*https://www.youtube.com/watch?v=NugRZGDbPFU.*

> Most new ideas come from rearranging and reconnecting different pieces of information.

Successful new ideas tend to come from things that we already know but have not yet connected. If an idea is too new or has too many unfamiliar elements, then typically the world is not ready for it and it fails to take off. While auction houses have existed for many years, it took personal computers and the internet to be in widespread use before eBay could be invented.

"Eureka!" moments, when a major new thought process happens, are mostly fictional. Discoveries tend to come at the end of long periods of research that may have involved many failures along the way. There is a long, slow process of discovery before that is reached, but in the euphoria of the moment, that is often forgotten.

Not many ideas come from just one person working alone. Most tend to come from people working together or from a network of people working on similar problems. This is where the expression, "standing on the shoulders of giants" comes from. Researchers benefit from all the work that has been done before their work in developing something new. The proliferation of easily available information that has come about with the internet has made this even more likely.

Serendipity, the idea of a happy accident, is often referenced when new ideas come along. It is the concept that while looking for one thing, something else was found. For example, the discovery of penicillin came from an accident. Scottish biologist Alexander Fleming was investigating staphylococci and went on holiday. When he returned, he found that one Petri dish had been left open and a blue-green mould had formed. This fungus had killed off all surrounding bacteria in the culture. The mould contained a powerful antibiotic, penicillin, that could kill harmful bacteria without having a toxic effect on the human body.

Other ideas come from using things for a different purpose than was originally envisaged. Apparently bubble wrap was first sold as a wallpaper! Marc Chavannes and Alfred Fielding created it through sealing together two shower curtains, which made the first layer of the bubbles. Not surprisingly, they were unsuccessful. It was only later that companies started to use it to keep products safe during shipping.

Finally, new ideas come from re-packaging existing ideas into different formats. Cassette players had existed for many years and were familiar to everyone. However, they were always large, often with integrated speakers. The idea of the Walkman, from Sony, just repackaged this, using smaller components, to form a personal, portable, music player.

Of course, some things do come from one person having a brilliant thought. The concept of Velcro came from a Swiss electrical engineer, George de Mestral, who wondered why burdock seeds clung to his coat and dog. His idea, that a fabric strip with tiny hooks could attach to another fabric strip with smaller loops, created a whole new way of fastening things. However, he still took an existing thing – burdock seeds – and made something new from it.

**Sales Ideas**

Sales opportunities come from knowing what your product does and what your customer is doing. By putting the two together, you are able to find opportunities.

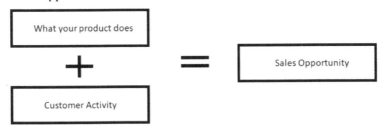

Figure 7.1     Creating a Sales Opportunity

This means that you must understand both in some detail. I am going to assume that you understand what your product does and the sorts of problems that it solves for customers. It is worth reviewing this on a regular basis to try to identify new uses for it. The more ideas that you have about how your product can be used, the more sales opportunities you will find.

You now have to consider what a potential customer might be doing that might make them develop a need for your product. Of course, not all companies will make it easy for you by announcing these sorts of changes. You may have to persuade them to change from their current way of working, which is another part of the sales effort. We discuss this more in Chapter 15, Why Change?

However, before we try to do that, we must understand some basic information about them. We have to do some primary research. This is similar to market research, although market research is directed to a whole market place, customer research is aimed towards individual customers within that market place.

**Market Research**

Market research is an organized effort to gather information about target markets or customers and to understand their wants, needs and beliefs. It provides important information which helps to identify and analyse the needs of the market, the market size and the competition. Market-research techniques encompass both qualitative techniques such as focus groups or interviews, as well as quantitative techniques such as customer surveys.

Market research can include:

1.  Market information such as the prices of different commodities in the market, as well as the supply and demand situation.
2.  Market segmentation or the division of the market or population into groups with similar motivations.
3.  Market trends – what is changing, during a period of time.
4.  SWOT analysis - Strengths, Weaknesses, Opportunities and Threats to a business entity.
5.  PEST analysis includes an examination of a company's Political, Economic, Social and Technological external factors which may impact a company's objective or profitability.
6.  Brand tracking which is a way of continuously measuring the health of a brand, both in terms of consumers' usage of it and what they think about it.

## Customer Research

Our customer research is similar to market research. We start with an idea of what types of customer might need our products based on our understanding of what the products can do. We will test this with them through market research and possibly refine our ideas over time based on the results of this research. So, how do we go about this?

Before we start our research, we have to know what we are looking for. Blindly trawling the web looking at random companies is not very efficient or effective. We have to know why a company would use the product that you are selling. This does not have to be too detailed but you must have some idea. For example, if you sell technology that specific scientists use, then your target companies must employ those specific scientists. If you sell technology for HR professionals, you must target companies with an HR department.

> You must know why a company would use the product that you are selling.

If you have a brand-new product, it is likely that it has been designed for a specific market place. In this case, it should be obvious who you are initially going to target. If the product has existed for some time, it is likely that your company will have made some sales in the past. To understand who might buy your product in the future, it is worth looking at the past to see what types of companies have previously bought it and why.

On a regular basis, it is worth reviewing what types of company are likely to use your product. You may have an idea of who would use it but sometimes customers can appear, almost out of nowhere, to ask about it, so try not to be too fixed on who would or would not use it. There may also be a range of factors that determine what companies to look for and some companies will be more suitable to you than others. We review all of this in the next chapter, What does a good customer look like? For now, we will review how to go about doing your research to help to start your analysis.

The purpose of our research is to determine whether a company is a potential customer or not.

The first step is to select a group of potential customers. This might be a specific type of company, for example all accountancy companies; this might be all the companies of a particular size; it might be all the companies in a particular area. You need to have some way of narrowing down all the companies in your territory to create a long list to review. The second step is to review each of these companies to try to determine if they might be a potential customer.

The obvious place to start to understand a company is its website. There are very few companies that do not have a website and it will give you all the basic information that you require to start with. For example:

- What is their main purpose?
- Where are they located?
- What do they produce?
- How are they organised?
- What types of people do they employ?

This should give you an initial impression of the company. Experienced sales people can often tell from just this information whether the customer is likely to want their products. For less experienced sales people, some more defined criteria will be helpful. This is something that will be specific to each company and probably to each product line within each company. I recommend building such a list using the collective knowledge of all of the sales team.

There are other places that are well worth looking for information before you go too much further.

1. LinkedIn is a great resource for finding out who works in a particular company. It will give you a feel for how many and what types of people work at the company. This can give you an idea of what the potential size of any deal might be.

2. Government Information Sites. Government websites will have basic information on all companies. This may include the names of all of the directors and financial information. This can be useful to determine the potential spending power of the company and who is ultimately responsible for spending it.

3. Industry Information Websites. In most industries, there are news and information services that detail activity in that sector. These are sometimes just a restatement of information on a company website but they usually cover all companies and countries so the information can be organised in a way that suits you. For example, if you want to find out which companies work in a particular country, then a good information service will usually provide that.

4. Conferences and Exhibitions. These are very good ways to get to know a company. At a conference, they will often present the results of their work which tells you what they are doing. At exhibitions, a company may have a booth detailing their activity and the people staffing the booth will generally be willing to tell you more. In addition, this can be a good way of meeting specific contacts. The other good thing about conferences and exhibitions is that there are multiple companies present so you can find out a lot of information about a lot of companies in a short space of time.

You should aim to understand the same basic information about each company so that you can start to target your efforts at the ones which you judge to be the most likely to buy. These are your good customers.

# 8

# WHAT DOES A GOOD CUSTOMER LOOK LIKE?

*"I can't give you a sure-fire formula for success, but I can give you a formula for failure: try to please everybody all the time."*
Herbert Bayard Swope

This is not a question of how they look physically – we really do not care if they are male, female, black, white, short or tall. The question is essentially, are they more likely to buy my product than another customer? It is highly unlikely that your company has sufficient sales resources to fully target every possible customer equally. It is also likely that not every company will be equally interested in your product at the same time. As a result, you have to prioritise your work and focus on the customers that are most likely to buy your product in the near future.

> You need to prioritise your work and focus on the customers that are most likely to buy your product in the near future.

All customers must be managed in some way but what you do will be different based on how likely they are to buy in the near future. All activities within the sales process must be done all of the time, although some will take more effort than others. The customers who are most likely to buy now should receive the most personal attention to move them to closure; we want to be proactive with these. The companies that are less likely to buy should be sent information, invited to technology workshops etc to build their understanding of your product and how it might benefit them; we want to be more reactive to these companies.

> At any given time, only 10% of your potential customers are actively buying products related to what you do.

Analysis indicates that at any given time only 10% of your potential customers are actively buying products related to what you do. The chances are that, unless they are actively talking to you, they are buying from someone else. As a result, trying to persuade them to buy your product is going to be an uphill struggle. Most customers, having made the decision to buy, quickly decide who they are going to buy from. From that point on, they are difficult to persuade to change without a compelling reason. Lots of companies will drop their prices significantly to try to win these sorts of deals and they may win a few but it is not a good model for long term business success. Having won at a very low price, it can be difficult to make much profit from such an agreement so the seller tries to cut their costs which can lead to poor service delivery and an unhappy customer. It can also lead to complications with other customers or for renewal business in that it is difficult to raise prices once they are that low. Much better to have recognised the potential for a sale early in the customer's buying process and won the deal at your preferred price.

Analysis also shows that 50% of potential customers are not ready to buy at all. They are generally quite happy with what they have and see no reason to change. Again, these are difficult customers to sell to. The mistake that most people make with these customers is to try to persuade them to buy their product. They are not interested in buying your product because they are happy as they are. You first have to persuade them to change what they are doing. Only once they have decided to change what they are doing, will they decide to buy something to help them. We discuss this more in Chapter 15, Why Change?

This leaves 40% of potential customers ready to buy. These are the ones that we want to be spending most of our time with. However, even these customers can be divided into good customers and not so good customers.

To explain the difference that targeting the right customer makes, consider the example of Meet the Adebanjos. This is a family based British sitcom centred on a British-African family living in Peckham, South London. The sitcom focuses on the larger than life father character Bayo Adebanjo as he struggles to instil his old fashioned, African values on his reluctant, modern, British family. Initially, the show creators made a number of pilot episodes and pitched it to mainstream stations in UK and US. However, it was not really the right show for those stations and was constantly rejected. However, when it was pitched to African television companies, all of a sudden, it was extremely popular and over 30 TV stations acquired the rights to broadcast it. It was also recently made available on Netflix.

The producers made the mistake of not thinking correctly about which TV stations would be the best for their product. They were based in UK so were keen for a UK station to acquire the rights. While the African TV stations would not pay as much as a UK TV company, there were many more of them. In addition, the characters in the sitcom are more interesting to people living in Africa than people living in UK.

> Regardless of what you are selling, you have to find the right companies to buy your product.

There are many further good reasons for targeting and working with good customers. We usually have a mutually beneficial relationship with our good customers and they generate lots of revenue for us. Poor customers can frequently cost us time and money and as a result, we should spend less time working with them. We may even decide not to deal with them at all if we decide that they are never likely to buy anything from us, regardless of how good our product is.

Poor customers waste our time, do not buy and are generally more trouble than they are worth.

They have some standard characteristics that help us to recognise them:

1. They are unresponsive;
2. They do not want to build a relationship;
3. They only ever buy the cheapest products;
4. They frequently change direction;
5. They are overly demanding;
6. They are indecisive.

All of these things waste our time and potentially waste our money. The customer could seem very keen on your product and ask lots of questions and get a lot of information out of you without ever intending to buy anything. They are just trying to learn something new. Most sales people want to help their customers and want to promote their products, so go along with this in the hope that the customer will buy. However, they seldom do and so are frustrating to deal with.

> When you do not have time to chase every customer, weeding out those who waste your time is an important exercise.

When I use the term "poor customer", I am really just meaning "not so good". It is all a relative scale, everyone could be a customer, some are just more likely to be a good customer today rather than others. So, we might phrase our distinction as firstly, are they ever going to be a good customer for my product? If so, then secondly, is this a good customer today or will they be a good customer in the future?

To illustrate this, I would like to introduce you to Dr Paddi Lund, the self-confessed "Crazy Dentist" from Queensland, Australia. A number of years ago, Paddi was an unhappy dentist with lots of customers he did not really like treating. He kept losing staff from his practice as they were not happy. One day, he decided to change all of that.

Paddi decided to put happiness at the front and centre of his business; the happiness of his customers, the happiness of his staff and his own happiness. You can read all about it on his website (www.paddilund.com) and in various books that he has written. For anyone looking to make positive changes to their business, I heartily recommend reading his books.

One of the changes that he made to his practice was to prioritise his customers. He applied the Pareto Principle (there are 80% of your customers who give you 20% of your revenue and 20% of your customers give you 80% of your revenue) to his customers. He realised that the time he spent with some customers was much more than they were paying for. He was actually paying them for the privilege of serving them.

He divided his customers into 4 categories – A, B, C and D's. 25% of people were great to deal with, complained little, appreciated the service that was provided, paid their bill in a timely fashion and thus gave him most of his profit. They were the A's. The B's were slightly deficient in one of those characteristics, the C's more so and the D's were the people who were quite undesirable to him. The A's gave him the most profit and pleasure; the D's, the most losses and pain. This was not a judgement on them as people but a judgement of how valuable they were for his business.

The 'D' people didn't particularly want the services that Paddi offered. He had to persuade them very hard to buy his services, they were not particularly grateful for them and would frequently complain afterwards.

Having categorised all of his customers. Paddi started to pay more attention to the A's and much less attention to the D's. When required, he would prioritise serving an A customer over any other. He even persuaded some of the D's to move to different practices. Over time, Paddi has worked to develop all of his customers to be A's so that he is only treating those people that he likes and that like him.

As a result, Paddi was able to remove all signs to his surgery and stop advertising. The only new customers he took on were referrals from existing "A" customers. After ringing the front door bell, all customers get greeted by their personal dental nurse and given tea or coffee while they wait. In return for staying with him, Paddi demanded that his customers did exactly as he asked in terms of looking after their teeth. In return, he promised them a pain free treatment. The result was that Paddi worked less and earnt more. He was happy and his customers were happy.

All of this came about by him getting rid of the customers that he did not want to treat and did not make him happy. While I am not suggesting that you immediately get rid of unwanted customers, deciding who you are going to focus your time and effort on is an important exercise to do so that you do not waste your time and money chasing poor customers.

In some respects, it can be quite easy to determine a good or not so good potential customer. I used to sell data related to the oil industry that was purely associated with countries in Africa. However, not all oil companies are working in Africa nor do they want to. As a result, it was quite easy for me to divide my potential customers into two categories, "working in Africa" and "not working in Africa". My good customers were obviously those in the first category and I could safely ignore the other companies for this product.

Conversely, a few years ago, a friend of mine was phoned up by a company selling conservatories and the salesman thought he was doing really well because my friend was really interested, said how much she would like one, kept the guy on the phone for about 15 minutes before he asked her for her address.

"Flat 8, 36 George Street" was the response.

"So, is that on the ground floor?" came back the question!

"No, on the second" was her response to which the salesman put the phone down.

Clearly my friend was not a good customer for a conservatory. Now, when the sales person called her, he could not possibly have known that she lived on the second floor so could not be a customer. However, he could have found it out very quickly and easily by asking about the property that she lived in. This is a very simple qualification question that too many people fail to ask up front.

Clearly, there will be a number of different factors that impact whether a customer is a good one or not and some will be more important than others. Consider geography and order size. A customer who is close to your office / factory is easier to service than one who is based tens of miles away, which in turn is better than one based hundreds of miles away. The closer a customer is, the easier it is to meet with them, deliver to them and work with then in whatever way that you have to. As a result, a customer who is based closer to you is better than a customer who is based further away.

The size of an average order is also a factor in determining a good customer. A customer who makes large orders is better than one who makes small orders; a customer who makes lots of orders is better than one who makes only a few orders. However, which is better, a customer who makes lots of small orders or one who makes a few large orders? Which is better, a customer who works nearby who makes a few orders or a customer further away who makes lots of orders?

> We have to determine which factors define how valuable a customer is and how important is each of these factors.

We must have some way of managing all of the different factors that determine whether or not our customer a good one or not. To that end, we have to determine which factors define how valuable each customer is and then how important is each of these factors. To do this, we use the table below.

| Criteria | What is the criterion? |
|---|---|
| Poor | What does a poor customer look like? What score does that equate to? |
| Good | What does a good customer look like? What score does that equate to? |
| Score | What score will you assign to this customer? |
| Comment | What is the reason for this |
| Action | What can you do to improve this score? |

Table 2: Ranking customers

For each criterion, you have to define what a good customer does and what a poor customer does. Each of these then has to have a score associated with it. By varying the maximum score, you effectively rank each of the criteria such that those that are more important give a bigger maximum score than those that are less important.

For example, you might decide that customers within 25 miles of your office are the most important ones for you and that this is worth 10 points. Customers more than 100 miles away are not good so are only worth a score of 4 points. The points differential does not have to be the maximum that it could be as a customer a long way away can still be worthwhile so should not be discounted.

For the size of order, you might determine that a customer that places orders worth £10,000 are the best ones and worth 10 points.

Conversely, customers that place orders worth less than £1,000 are barely worth the effort and therefore only worth 1 point.

You might have a further criterion about other factors such as paying bills. Customers who pay on time might earn 5 points and customers who you have to chase each month for payment might only earn 1 point. A maximum score of 5 demonstrates that while this criterion is a factor in whether the customer is good or not, the factor is not as important as geography or order size.

When you consider each customer, they will score somewhere between the maximum and minimum score for each criterion. A customer that is 50 miles from the office might score 5 points, if they place orders worth £6,000 they might earn 6 points and lastly if they pay their bills within 30 days they score an additional 5 points. They then have a total score of 16 points. When all customers are scored using the same criteria, you can then rank them all against each other.

The final column of the table is an action. This defines any action that you could take to improve the score. Clearly, the location of the customer is not something that you can have any impact on. If a customer fails to pay bills on time, it might be worth meeting with them to try to understand why. Clearly, they have agreed to pay on time but are not doing so for some reason. If you can understand that, you might be able to change things such that they do pay on time and then they receive a higher score as a result.

A worked example is included in the Examples at the end of the book.

Once this process has been done for all customers, you must then review all of the results. This graph shows the raw results for a sample set of customers, simply tabulated and graphed in Excel. In this instance, the maximum score was 100.

Figure 8.1: Ranking Customers 1

It is then possible to order the results from lowest to highest to determine the priority for working with each customer.

Figure 8.2: Ranking Customers 2

In this example, all of the customers scoring over 60 points have been classed as great. These are your best customers and the ones that you should be focussing on as a priority. You have to nurture them and build the relationship with them so that they continue to be great customers.

There are a large number of customers scoring between 50 and 60 points who can be classified as good customers. These are ones to be chased as a second priority but which could, with some work, be classified as great.

Finally, there are the lowest scoring customers who may be treated as transactional customers. If they contact you, then you will work with them but you will not go out of your way to chase work from them. Of course, there may be some simple activities that you can do to try to boost their score but in the main, these potential customers will be ignored for most of the time.

There are some other considerations to this analysis.

1. Each customer might rank differently for different product lines.
2. This is a continuous process; you have to revisit the ranking on a regular basis.
3. Try to be as objective as possible to ensure you are consistent.
4. It is a small world – people move between companies and if they have been positive or negative about your products then they will take that belief with them.

If you have a wide range of products, then you will deal with a wide variety of groups and people within those groups and some may be more disposed to you than others. You may have a large install base in one part of the business but not in another. The part where you have no business may be a great opportunity and therefore the customer might rank highly or it may be a closed shop to you in which case, they may rank low for that product line. How you divide things is up to you but do not assume that every customer is the same for every product. You may have to do the analysis per product line to ensure that you continually focus on the right customers for the right product.

> Each solution requires its own analysis and potentially each solution in each country requires its own analysis. These should be revised annually to account for changes within each company.

Things change, people change, needs change. A good customer one day may become a less attractive customer the next. You do not have to revise things every day but certainly every year you will want to review this analysis and determine who to focus on for that year. To that end, you should review and revise the analysis at a minimum of once per year, possibly twice per year.

It is very easy to be swayed by personal preferences or liking a particular person within a company. This should be avoided if possible because they are not the best criteria to work with. It is easy to get meetings with some customers but be realistic about whether they will actually buy from you. Similarly, you might really want to win work with a particular company but for the wrong reasons. As a result, you should try to be as objective as possible. To that end, you should have the same person complete all of the analysis for a specific country, product or set of customers to avoid bias and ensure a consistent analysis.

Finally, while it is important to focus your efforts on your best customers, that does not mean that you should do nothing or fail to respond to the customers who do not rank highly. Companies get bought, people move from one company to the next and they take their preferences with them. The companies ranked near the bottom still have to be nurtured even if you do not spend lots of time on them. Think about ways that you can stay in touch with them in case they do change their behaviour and keep supporters within those companies onside for when they move positions or companies. Use ideas from The Science of Persuasion, Chapter 4, Selling throughout the Process.

# 9

# HOW TO GET THROUGH THE FRONT DOOR

*"You never really understand a person until you consider things from his point of view."*

Harper Lee

T
he hardest thing any sales person ever has to sell is their initial contact. Most people are too busy and focussed on what they have to do today to take notice of a new contact. Even when you call them directly, they will typically choose to reject the approach. This is not because they do not have problems or that they are not interested, they just do not understand why they should be interested. We discuss handling objections more in Chapter 20, Negotiations. However, this initial rejection is not really an objection. The customer does not know enough to object.

Your first contact with a customer is always potentially difficult. Cold calling, in whatever form you use, is difficult, even for people with many years of experience. You have to find some way of gaining the attention of the customer and then explaining why they should listen to you for a couple of minutes while you sell them the next stage of the process. At this stage, all you want to do is to get to the next stage, whatever that is. You do not want to try to sell your product, you want to sell a meeting or a longer call or maybe to persuade them to give you the name of the best person to talk to, preferably with a recommendation.

To get in with a new customer, you have to do two things within a couple of minutes of first contacting them. The first thing is to grab their attention to the extent that they agree to listen to you for the next stage of the call. The second thing is to say enough to get them interested in what you do so that they agree to a meeting to discuss it further or whatever you want your next stage to be. You must give them something of value to start to establish credibility and trust.

> When contacting a new customer, you have to gain their attention and tell them something valuable that will persuade them to listen to you further.

Initiating a contact is much easier with people that you know. They will usually be prepared to listen to you as you have hopefully earnt their respect in the past. They will give you some time because of this. However, you still have to tell them why listening to you is going to be worthwhile. They will be happy to answer your call and you do not have to grab their attention too much. However, if they detect that you are wasting their time, they probably will not let you get any further than that.

In the same way, people that you are recommended to will give you some time to make your point. While you may not have met them, the recommendation of a friend or colleague goes a long way to buying you some time. This is why so many companies meet with others via business networking groups. LinkedIn is also a way of connecting with people and establishing some trust before you ever contact them directly. If you are regularly posting articles and useful information, contacts will see this and build a positive impression of you before you establish a real relationship with them.

**Attracting Attention**

There is a great scene in one of my favourite movies, The Shawshank Redemption, demonstrating how to attract attention. *https://youtu.be/njJ41irPjTc* if you want to watch it.

A group of prison inmates is working on a roof in the jail when they overhear one of the wardens moaning about having inherited money and having to pay tax on it. The main character in the movie, Andy Dufresne, was an accountant and goes up to the warden and asks "Do you trust your wife?" This definitely attracts the warden's attention and Andy nearly gets thrown off the roof as a result. Fortunately, he has enough time to explain, that the warden can give the money to his wife and avoid the tax, so he avoids being thrown off the roof!

This was a very dramatic way of gaining attention but it worked and gave him the opportunity to explain how he could help him. It is not a line that I recommend using to a potential customer but the format of grabbing attention and then explaining how you can help is definitely one to follow.

You do not always have to be too explicit about how you can help. It is often sufficient to suggest that you can help, or suggest that the customer may be missing out on something that is enough to warrant a further meeting.

Many years ago, while working for a software company in the oil industry, I left the following voicemail for the exploration manager of a potential customer.

"Hi John, this is Tim Gibbons from ABC Software. Your company is the only major oil company in Aberdeen that does not have any ABC products in use so I am really keen to come to talk to you to discuss how we can help you with your exploration activities."

Typically, people in these sorts of roles never respond, no matter what they promise in their voicemail messages. However, on this occasion, the exploration manager called me back. I have to admit that I nearly fell off my chair when he did. This was so unexpected. What I had said had intrigued him enough to want to know more so we arranged to have a meeting where I could explain how I thought that our software could help him and his team.

**How do you grab your potential customer's attention?**

Most people already have a way of doing the work that they are required to do or a product to help them perform various tasks. Seldom does a ground breaking technology come along that does something entirely new. Smart phones are an example of new technology that changed the way that people work so were relatively easy to sell when they were first released. However, newer versions of smart phones are more difficult as they just enhance that experience rather than change things.

Even if a customer has a known problem or need, it is likely that they have an idea of how they are going to solve it. They may have done some research to investigate possible solutions or they have a preferred supplier that they think can help them. As a result, they have an opinion about the solution and people are very slow to change their opinions. They tend to reject information that does not fit with their view.

If you contact a potential customer who you believe might have a need that you can help with, simply offering a different product can therefore be quite difficult. The customer's in-built bias will tend to reject information that does not conform to their view. As a result, you must provide information that they do not know which either changes how they see the problem or provides different ways of solving it. Whatever you do, you must tell them something that they do not already know.

> When you first contact a client, you should try to tell them something that they do not already know.

Any time that we are presented with information that we do not know, we tend to stop and think. For example, in England, pigeon poo is property of the Crown! This is because pigeon poo could be used to make gunpowder. Because of this, King George I declared all pigeon poo to be property of the Crown in the 18th Century. Another fact that you probably did not know is that the pH scale was invented by the Carlsberg brewery. It was the brainchild of one Søren Sørensen who invented it in 1909 while researching the best proteins, amino acids and enzymes in the Carlsberg brewery laboratory. Both of those facts I found on a website so they could easily be fabricated, I honestly do not know! However, I knew neither of them before googling "amazing facts" and I found them interesting enough to make use of them here!

Of course, neither of these facts is very relevant for most sales calls so what sort of information can you give to your potential customer to persuade them to listen to you for a few minutes? To be sure that you are saying something relevant, you have to have researched your customer and know something about what they are doing and why they might be interested to hear what you have to say.

Some options include:

1.  You might open with some research or analysis that is relevant to their business. This must be very up to date to ensure that it is new information for the customer. If it is research that you

or your company has done, then that is often a great opening as this is quite likely to be new to your customer.

2. Consider stating some insight into how the use of your products have helped to solve business problems. Ensure that the problems are ones that the customer is likely to be suffering from.

3. If you have developed new ways of working or new best practise methodologies, these are also good openings. This is information that only you are knowledgeable of and can deliver as insight and training to your potential customer.

4. Introduce unconsidered needs to the customer. That is, unforeseen problems, challenges or missed opportunities that they may have underappreciated or do not yet know about that create flaws or limitations in their current approach.

> Ensure that you tell your customer something relevant to their business and their likely business needs.

Whichever of these you choose, ensure that the content is as relevant as possible to that customer. Do not talk about improvement in the manufacture of golf clubs to companies that work in recruitment, for example. Obviously, that is an extreme example but make whatever you say as relevant as you can to the customer you are talking to.

In addition, avoid using cheesy or gimmicky statements that might not form the best impression on your prospective customer. They might work for television commercials but they generally do not work in selling to businesses. Finally, and very definitely, do not make claims that are patently false or could be easily disproved. Assume that your customer is intelligent and up to date on information about their business. They are likely to spot dubious claims for what they are and they will not continue the conversation as a result.

**How do you present the information?**

There are a variety of ways that you can present the information to your customer. In addition, your customer will have a preference to receive information and communications in certain formats and styles. Until you get to know them, it is difficult to know what style they would prefer. We discuss this in some more detail in Chapter 18,

Different Buyers. Once you do know them, try to fit with their preferred style of communication.

Stories and analogies are two of the best ways of communicating when you have no prior knowledge of the customer's preferences. I have referenced the power of stories already and these are by far the best way of communicating in general. However, it can be difficult to start telling a business story to someone that you have never met within a minute of them answering the phone to you. Unless you can get to the business point very quickly, you run the risk of your customer losing interest in what you are saying.

An analogy is a bit like a story and has the advantage of generally being shorter. A good analogy makes us look at the problem in a different way. An analogy, or an analogue, is a comparison between two different things. For example, a map is a 2D representation of a 3D world. No one would ever suggest that looking at a map is the same as looking at the scene around us but the map is extremely useful in helping us to navigate through that scenery. Think about all of the terminology associated with desktop computers, such as files, folders, recycle bin etc. They are all words that we associate with a physical desktop and allow us to be more quickly comfortable with a digital desktop. There is a good video on YouTube all about analogies - https://www.youtube.com/watch?v=CvnmU2JGUHg.

By making a comparison between two things that are not the same, you are making your customer think and, more importantly, by making them think differently, they should reject their possible negative thoughts about what you have to offer. A good analogy is also far more interesting than a set of facts and, in the same way as a story, the customer should remember it much more than a list of facts that you might quote about their business.

**How do you contact them?**

There are a number of ways that you can reach out to a potential customer. Each has positive and negative aspects. You could send them a letter, send them an email, call them directly, connect with them on social media or meet them through some sort of networking event. In each case, you want to ensure that you follow the formula of grabbing their attention and then telling them something that they do not know to generate interest.

Let us consider each one individually:

**Send them a letter.** Many years ago, this was probably the only way that you could easily indirectly contact a customer. Today, it is quite unusual to use this method and for that reason, it could be effective. However, to get a response, it requires the customer to take action so it must be very appealing in order for that to happen. Even if the letter is appealing, it requires the most effort to respond so can end up being rejected. A letter is a good way of gently informing the customer about what you have to offer so that when you call them, they have some idea what you are talking about.

**Send them an email.** This is very much like sending a letter except that it is easier for the customer to respond. As many of your customers will receive tens, if not hundreds, of emails every day, your email must be very appealing in order to gain a response. Research suggests that sending an email is the most effective way of approaching a customer in terms of gaining a response. However, it is still only effective about 30% of the time. Again, it is a good way of informing the customer about what you have to offer so that when you call them, they have some idea what you are talking about.

**Connect with them on social media.** This is really just a way of warming up your customer to a more direct approach. By connecting with them on LinkedIn, you give them the chance to learn who you are and what you do in an indirect way, assuming that you are both active on the site. I suggest that you do not connect with a potential customer on other sites, unless they are dedicated to networking or are specific to your industry. Being active on LinkedIn requires you to be posting on a regular basis, at least weekly, if not twice weekly, so that irregular visitors can catch your activity. This gives your potential customer the chance to get to know you before you approach them directly. Do not expect much to come directly to you after each post. You are trying to build up trust in what you do in order to make progress when you initiate contact. Use comments etc on your posts to further build your network so that you have greater reach.

**Networking.** This can be an effective way of meeting people and is something that you should be doing as often as possible with your target market. There are many events that you can attend, such as exhibitions, conferences and specific networking events. These are good ways to meet new people but not the right environment for direct selling. The events are there to enable you to meet people and for them to start to trust you. If you focus on gaining their trust, then you will be more successful at gaining their business when you ask for it. It makes it a lot easier to call them after you have met them, than if you have not met them. Attend the events armed with useful information, stories and analogies to help to demonstrate your value and always follow up with new connections afterwards. The people that you meet may not need your product immediately but you want them to remember you for the time that they do need you. They may also introduce you to people who do immediately need your product.

> Prepare a variety of opening statements that can gain your customer's attention and make them want to listen to you.

**Call them.**

By far and away, this is the most effective way of contacting your customer and getting them to agree to listen to you. When you call them, it is difficult for them to avoid responding and they will generally talk to you for a couple of minutes at the very least. Before you call, plan what you are going to say. Your voice and your words are your only methods of communication at this time so you must have a good idea what you are going to say. Always ask for permission to continue the call once you have introduced yourself. If it is not convenient for the customer, ask them for a time that you can call back. If you do not manage to talk to them but you can leave a voice mail, do so once. More than once is a bit like stalking! Ensure that what you say is appealing and interesting. You should not expect a call back but your message will have warmed them up a bit. You will probably have to continue to call to finally get to talk to them. I suggest only calling once per day; again, calling too often can be off putting. When you do finally speak, ensure that you ask for something at the end of the call. Whether this is a further call at a more convenient time or a longer face to face meeting, know what you want to achieve before you call and ask for it. However, be prepared to accept a fallback position if you end up asking for too much.

> Know what you want to achieve from every connection and ensure that you agree a next step before you end the contact.

# 10

## PRESENTATIONS

*"It usually takes me more than three weeks to prepare a good impromptu speech."*

Mark Twain

No matter what you are selling or how you are selling it, you are likely to have to make presentations at some stage during your sales process. Whether you are selling directly to another business or trying to persuade another retailer to stock your product, you have to make a sales pitch. Presentations are not just delivered with PowerPoint. They could be a demonstration of a technology, a tour of a new building or facilities or an illustrated speech. Whatever the format, it is an important element of the sales process.

The presentation combines all elements of The Equation of Sales. Typically, you will be speaking to a wider audience than you have been communicating with previously. You have to form a good impression and build trust with each member of the audience. The audience is judging you as much as they are judging your product.

> A poorly presented product is less likely to be accepted than a well-presented product, no matter how good that product is.

Your presentation is likely to include proof that you can do what you are claiming. This might be by presenting previous successful work or by demonstrating your product. Proof is a critical part of the offer to your customer – all the words in the world cannot compete with seeing it in action. As the saying goes, "the proof of the pudding is in the eating". Making sure that your demonstration works, regardless of the format, is very important.

Lastly, a sales presentation is about making an offer to the customer. It should effectively mimic your proposal. You can read more about proposals in Chapter 19, Proposals. As such, the presentation is your chance to demonstrate what you have learnt about the customer and how you are going to help them. A great presentation will lead directly to a sale. Fail to deliver and you will be struggling to get the opportunity closed.

So, no matter who you are or what you sell, making great presentations is critical to your success. However, standing in front of an audience and making presentations is not something that many people are good at without some preparation and practise. Indeed, even the people who are great presenters have done a lot of preparation and practise.

Fear of public speaking and presentations is fairly common. You are not alone if the thought of speaking in public scares you. Presenting or speaking to an audience regularly tops the list in surveys of people's top fears - more than heights, flying or dying. There is a saying "most people would rather be in the coffin than delivering the eulogy." However, with preparation and practise, most people can become very competent at this. For those that do, the reward will be immense, not only in successfully closing deals but in reducing the stress that goes with this part of the role. So, what makes a good presentation?

A good presentation is interesting, informative and engaging. It is simple enough for everyone to understand. It keeps our attention no matter what other distractions there are in the room. A good presentation is like a good book. A great story book is one that we can hardly bear to put down. We read it rather than doing anything else because we want to know what happens. So, very simply, a great presentation is a story. A story that engages us, keeps us interested and makes us want more. If you can build your presentation as a story, you will be well on your way to being successful.

> A good presentation is like a good story; it engages us, keeps us interested and makes us want more.

A marketing presentation comes near the start of the sales process. In this type of presentation, you are just informing your potential customer of what you do as a way of leading into a discussion about their needs. It is important that the discussion follows immediately after the presentation so ensure that you schedule sufficient time for it. The content can mostly be the same for all customers as the presentation is much more focussed on your company and products rather than the customer.

A sales presentation comes towards the end of the sales process once you know everything that you have to know about your customer. It is essentially a presentation of your proposal and the proof that you can deliver it. It should be focussed specifically on that customer and detail their needs, your product, the benefits of your product and the proof that you can deliver. The next step after this should be a negotiation of the final deal.

A sales presentation should be focussed on your customer and their needs; it should detail your product, its benefits and the proof that you can deliver.

# Needs

Definition (from Oxford English Dictionary)

1. (n) Circumstances requiring some course of action.
2. (n) Necessity for presence or possession of
3. (n) Thing wanted, respect in which want is felt, requirement

# 11

## NEEDS ANALYSIS

*"In seeking the truth, you have to get both sides of the story."*
Walter Cronkite

I believe that no business buys something that they do not need. It is the role of the sales person to identify those needs, propose a solution that involves their products and then get the customer to want those products. As a result, identifying those needs is one of the most critical things that a sales person does.

**Needs versus Wants**

Children will frequently state that they need something, usually the latest toy or game or, as they get older, particular clothes etc. What they really mean is that they want that thing. A need is something that you must have in order to survive. A want refers to something that would be nice to have but is not essential.

In pre-historic times, humans had three basic needs; food, shelter and clothing. Over time, we might add education and healthcare to this list. Maslow's Hierarchy of Needs is a five-tier model of human needs, with physiological needs (food, water, warmth, rest) at the bottom and self-actualisation (achieving one's full potential) at the top. Our basic needs are the things that keep us healthy and safe and if we do not have them, then illness and possibly death may result. Fortunately, our needs are limited and do not really change over time.

Figure 11.1: Maslow's Hierarchy of Needs

Once our basic needs are met, further "needs" are mainly things that are nice to have or a "want". They are things that a person would like to possess, either immediately or at a later time. We will still survive if we do not get them, although we might not be as happy as we would be if we had them. These wants may vary from person to person and from time to time. Our wants are essentially unlimited. What limits us is the means to acquire them.

In business, it is more difficult to make this distinction. A business can be formed with only the very basic of requirements. Many are formed in a garage or a shed with someone making a prototype of an idea that they have had. Consultancies often start in a spare room or even a coffee shop. However, as they start to grow, they start to need more things. Once a few people are employed, they generally need premises to work from; they may need desks and computer equipment or a machine to manufacture goods. Theoretically, all of these are wants as the business was able to function without them to begin with. However, in order to grow, develop and make more profits, the business wants to buy these items and so in reality, they are things that the business needs.

In many cases, the people within the business are well aware of the things that they need. Like human needs, they can change over time. As the business grows, it might move from doing all accounting on a spreadsheet to an online system that also calculates VAT returns and corporation tax. As demand for a product grows, new manufacturing capabilities might be needed. These needs will come from the growth of the business and should be fairly obvious to the business managers. In these instances, they may approach the market with a list of needs and ask for proposals to help them.

However, not all needs will be obvious to a business as they may not be aware of what is possible. For example, a new data processing technique may make customer data analysis much quicker but unless the business is aware of the technique, they may never be aware of how much they need it. This is where a sales person can make the most impact as they can persuade the customer to change and adopt a new process that uses the technology that the sales person provides. We discuss how to drive change in Chapter 15, Why Change? Of course, the sales person can only do this if they can recognise the need for change in the customer.

**Needs Analysis**

A Needs Analysis is a process for identifying and evaluating developments that should be done.  Needs are often referred to as gaps or the difference between what is currently done and what should be done.  It is quite often used in terms of learning and development to define how to improve the skills of a team through training.  The US Department of Education defines a "need" as the difference between the way things are and the way they should be.

> A need is the difference between the way things are and the way that they should be.  All businesses have them and will buy products to satisfy that need.

For example, consider a business that decides to review the time that it takes to build a particular component.  They discover that it takes them five days.  In itself, this information does not do much for them.  However, if they then discover that their competitor can build the same component in three days, then they can immediately see that they are at a competitive disadvantage and may lose orders and revenue as a result.  They have to determine how to reduce their manufacturing time to three days in order to be competitive.

A business needs analysis (BNA) is an analysis tool that helps a company to identify the key drivers for change and to determine the best options or solutions to resolve needs or improve productivity or performance. The purpose of the business needs analysis is to clearly understand the business and its needs.  There are a variety of ways that a business might go about doing this.  These include:

- SWOT analysis.  SWOT stands for Strengths, Weaknesses, Opportunities and Threats.  The business will list out each of them and then determine activities that can be done to minimise or eliminate their weaknesses and take advantage of their opportunities.
- Gap analysis.  This process looks at what a business is trying to achieve and what it is actually achieving.  The gaps between them are used to define the activities that have to happen to close these gaps.

- Benchmarking. This looks at the results that a business is achieving and compares them to competitors. Where a business is at a disadvantage, for example in processing time, then action can be taken to improve.

- Capability analysis. This is similar to benchmarking in that a business looks at its core competencies and reviews their abilities or maturity level in each of them. This identifies areas of the business that can be improved and action can be taken to improve.

- Variance analysis. In this analysis, the business looks at what its forecast or ideal performance is and what its actual performance is. This is frequently done by sales organisations! From there, they can start to review what can be done better and how they will go about doing this.

- Problem analysis. Here a company will look at where their processes have broken down or failed. Analysis will seek to determine the root cause of the problem and identify changes that can prevent future failures. This is very common in manufacturing processes.

- Requirements analysis. The people working within an organisation can often see problems that management might not see. By collecting ideas from all stakeholders, a business can further identify areas for improvement.

It is quite likely that a business will have many needs and may not be able to address all of them at the same time. They will have to prioritise needs and work on them in order of priority.

One important factor that determines the priority of a need is what the consequences will be if the need is not met. For example, failing to improve a manufacturing time might lead to the loss of many customers and the associated revenue which could cause the entire business to fail. This is therefore a high priority. The other important factor in determining priority is how easy the problem is to fix. If it can be fixed with a simple process change then it is likely to get fixed quicker than if it requires a major new piece of machinery to be purchased. Of course, there is a balance between these two factors. If the lack of expensive machinery could lead to the loss of all customers, then clearly that will be more important than a simple process change that saves a few hundred pounds each month.

All of this work will be done regularly by a business and will be an important and confidential analysis that is kept within the business. It will drive a lot of activity and consequent spending by the company. As a result, it is like gold dust to a sales person! Where a sales person is completely trusted by a business, aspects of the analysis may be shared with them. Businesses recognise that a good sales person is like a partner and wants them to be successful. This is why it is so important for a sales person to be trusted by a business.

If the business does the needs analysis and approaches a sales person for help, then they are likely to have already decided what they need. This can be great as it can result in an easy sale and who does not like them! However, if the opposite occurs and you are not able to provide a solution that fixes their immediate problems, then it will be difficult to make a sale as you are not solving their most important problems. In this case, it is better to give them the time to solve their most important problems, stay in touch and come back when they are ready to solve the problems that you are able to help them with.

> To be successful, a sales person has to identify the possible needs that a company has and how they can help the company to meet those needs.

Having said all of this, it is highly likely that a business will keep its needs to itself and give little indication of what they are. As a result, for a sales person to be successful, they have to be able to identify what those needs might be. If they can identify these, then they can approach the customer to find out more and work towards providing a solution. Identifying these needs is the most important thing that a sales person does. If they get it right, they make sales. Get it wrong and they lose sales and possibly worse! So, let us consider needs a bit more.

**Identifying Needs**

No business buys something that they do not believe that they need. They may or may not be aware of that need before the sales person calls but if they cannot see that need, then the sale is highly unlikely to happen.

This really cannot be stressed enough. No matter how great your product is, if your potential customer does not see a need for it, then they are not going to buy it. I used to work for a company that sold seismic data. This data is used to identify where oil and gas may be located under the ground. At a trade show, one of my colleagues tried to convince an oil company executive to consider exploring for oil in a particular African country because our company had really great data in that country. Now, the decision to explore in any country is made on the basis of many, many factors. Some countries are easier to work in than others. The quantity and quality of data available is one of those factors but it is very low down the list and no one is going to make the decision to start to work in a country based solely on the quality of data available. As a sales technique, it was not one of the best!

So, before they ever approach a company, a sales person has to identify firstly whether the company meets their criteria for a good customer and secondly, can they identify a potential reason for them to need their product. You can never be completely sure of these needs before you actually go and ask them but you want to be sure enough that you are asking a sensible question in the first place. You could go and just ask them "what do you need?" but that is a very cold, logical question and does not really get the best results. It is much better to ask about their objectives and activities before leading on to their needs. We will discuss questioning techniques in the next chapter. In order to be able to discover their needs, you must have an idea what their activities are which may lead to their specific need for your product.

The purpose of our customer research is to review a company's activities to determine if they have the potential to be a customer. For many years, I have sold software that is used almost exclusively by geophysicists. So, during my research, I had to understand if my potential customer employed geophysicists and if so, how many. There was more that I needed to know before I could make a sale but the starting point was "Do they employ geophysicists?" From there, I looked at the areas of the world where the company was working to see if there were specific problems that could be solved using the technology that I sold. This enabled me to identify specific uses for the software that I could highlight to persuade the company to buy. This was then my starting point for my conversation with the company.

A customer's need is identified by some form of needs analysis that defines what they are doing and what they would like to be doing or what they are doing / not doing compared to their competitors. There are two steps in this process. Firstly, you have to look at all of the possible reasons (Generic Needs) why a customer might use your product. This will help to identify the areas (Specific Needs) to look for in specific customers that will help to inform you if they need your products.

**Generic Needs**

To be able to recognise how a customer will benefit from your product, you have to understand how they are going to use it. In general, a company will buy a product to improve their business; this frequently means either to be able to do things faster or to do things with less resources. In certain industries, such as the oil industry or anything that uses heavy machinery, improving safety and reducing the risk of accidents is also a very important reason to do things differently.

Most processes that technology improves can be done without that technology. It is perfectly possible to make a cake without a food processor. However, the food processor improves the speed with which we can mix the ingredients and so we can make a cake faster. If our business is all about making cakes, then a food processor is an obvious machine to buy. As the business grows, we can either buy more food processors or one larger food processor. Either way, as the business evolves, its needs will change.

A very simple example is for a smart phone, particularly when they were first introduced and were not so common. In simple terms, a smart phone makes telephone calls, can access the internet and send and receive emails. Clearly it does a lot more but for the sake of this example, we will restrict it to these. For someone sitting at a desk in an office, they can do all of these things with a computer so if they sit at the same desk all day, every day, then they probably do not need one. However, if someone is regularly out of the office and needs to make calls and receive emails, then a smart phone is a very useful tool.

In this instance, we understand what a smart phone does but it is not sufficient to simply state that a potential user is someone who needs to make calls and send emails. The mobile aspect is critical to identifying the real need. So, we can state that the generic needs of a customer for a smart phone are to make calls and send emails while out of the office.

This is a simple example and it is likely that your potential customers will have many complex needs and reasons why they might need your product. However, it is important to try to recognise as many of them as possible. The simplest way to think about this is to think of what and when a customer is likely to use your product.

A very simple workflow that generates a sale can be defined as:

1. Customer attempts process A
2. During process A, customer encounters a problem that prevents its completion
3. Customer buys product from supplier to solve the problem
4. Customer successfully completes process A.

The task of product managers and sales people is to identify all of the possible processes that a customer is doing that might result in them buying the particular product that they are offering. Ask yourself the questions:

1. What might a company be doing to make them need to buy your products?
2. What are they going to do once they have access to the product?

If your product solves a particular problem, then any company that is likely to have this problem is likely to need your product.

At this stage, you can be fairly general about their needs. You are considering a generic company so consider generic reasons. Once you have these, you can move on to the specific needs of a specific customer.

**Specific Needs**

We started to understand our customer during our Customer Research in Chapter 7. This gave us a basic understanding of what they are doing and where. We now want to extend that research to identify specific needs that will allow us to sell our product to them.

There is a variety of ways that we might start to identify a specific need in a company. They may only be tentative ideas but they provide us with sufficient information to be able to contact that company and start a conversation. The obvious place to start is with the generic reasons and find specific instances of these workflows within the company.

There are a variety of ways that we might identify specific needs.

**They just need it.** In order to do certain activities, certain products are needed and not all of them last forever. For example, to drill an oil well, you need a drilling rig and a drill bit – just as if you were drilling a hole in the wall at home. The specific geology that you are drilling through will influence the type of drill bit that you need but however you look at it, if you are going to drill a well, then you need a drill bit. This means that it is relatively easy for the drill bit sales person as they just have to know who is going to be drilling a well. This is information that is readily available from various information services so this specific need is easy to identify. If this is the case for you, identifying your prospective customers and their needs are fairly straight forward.

**What do our other customers do?** If one customer has used your product to improve their business, then other companies that do the same thing are equally likely to need your product. I highly recommend talking to existing customers on a regular basis to find out how they are using your product and then applying that knowledge to other customers. Users are extraordinarily good at using technology in ways that were not anticipated by the manufacturers. I recall being at a long-stay airport car park and seeing someone taking a photo with their smartphone of where their car was parked. As someone who has once "lost" a car in a massive, featureless car park, I completely understood why they were doing that. However, I do not expect for a minute that the phone designer ever expected the phone to be used for that reason.

> The more that you know about how your product is used, the more that you can tell others how they can benefit from it.

**Closeology.** This is a word made up by a friend and it refers to what others are doing nearby. In the oil industry, companies are allocated areas of the land or sea, known as blocks, to explore for oil in. They have the right to work there and no one else does. However, the geology of the area does not change very fast so the geology of one block is very similar to the geology of the next. As a result, if your company provides products to a company in one block to help to solve a particular problem, it is quite likely that the company in the block next door also has the same problem. They are an obvious candidate for a sales call. These are great customers to find as you have a success story to tell them when you go to see them. Not only do you understand their problem but you know how to solve it and can prove it.

**Analogues**. In a similar fashion, if you have helped another customer to solve a specific problem, then can you see which of your potential customers also might have this problem. For example, there are a lot of companies that provide information services such as legal and regulatory information and analytics. While all accountancy and legal companies need this information, it is not practical for them to gather all of it themselves. It is much easier for one company to do this and sell the product to others. As the provider talks to its customers, they will find out the problems that they are solving using the product and can then talk to other customers about it in order to sell or extend their products with them.

All of these ways of identifying needs can be summarised in one word – experience. For someone new to selling a particular product, it can be difficult to identify potential customer needs. With experience, this becomes easier until you get to the stage where it just seems obvious. As a result, it is worth working with more experienced sales people in your team to try to identify needs once you have determined that you have a good potential customer. Working in groups is always a more effective way of doing this as the interaction between people can help to develop more ideas than just one person alone.

If you have a relatively new product, it is quite possible that your customer will need it but will have no idea that they need it. For example, there is a new tablet that allows you to write on it to take handwritten notes and convert them into text. (https://remarkable.com/ in case you are interested!) This has not really been possible to date and for someone or a company that does a lot of hand written note taking, it can replace paper and save a lot of time. However, if you do not know that it exists, then you could never see the need for one. In this instance, the sales person must introduce the product to the customer before they can make progress. Depending on the type of product, this activity is generally led by marketing, for horizontal markets, or by business development in vertical markets.

**Insufficient knowledge**

At the end of your needs gathering exercise, it is quite likely that you will not be 100% certain that your customer can benefit from your product. In order to be confident that your customer needs your product, you will have to find out more information and the only way to do that is to go to ask them about their existing projects or workflows to determine if the need really exists.

You should have a good idea of what information you must know in order to be able to write a proposal. With the information that you have, you will be able to see what information you still have to find. This should therefore start to define the list of questions that you will ask the customer when you get to meet them. We will look at this in more detail in the next chapter.

# 12

## ASKING QUESTIONS

*"Judge a man by his questions rather than his answers"*
Voltaire

During our research, we will have found out a variety of facts about our customer and some of their needs. However, this will not be enough to understand all of their needs and determine if they require our products. We must meet with them and find out more. This is a critical part of the sales process as it starts our personal interaction with the customer.

To be successful, you will first have to make contact and generate some interest in the mind of the customer. This is covered in Chapter 5, Building Trust, and Chapter 9, How to Get Through the Front Door. So, assuming that you have done this successfully, you will have a reasonably receptive audience with your customer and the opportunity to make progress. Like any stage of the sales process, you must plan what you are going to do. As this is the point where you meet the customer for the first time, this is a very important part to plan carefully.

**Meeting Planning**

The first thing to do is to know who you are going to meet and find out more about them. What is their role? Might they have specific individual needs that you have to consider as well as those of the company. Have you met them before or do you know someone in common? If you have not met them before, look them up on LinkedIn or other such forums to find out about them.

I once went into a meeting and met someone that I had worked with about 20 years previously. He remembered me although was not sure where we had met before. However, I did not remember him and felt at a complete disadvantage throughout the meeting. It made the conversation difficult as a result. Once I left the meeting, I looked him up on LinkedIn and remembered exactly where I had worked with him.

Even if you have not met the customer before, you may know people in common or may have common interests. This is a great way of starting the conversation with them in a soft, non-business way which helps to build rapport and trust.

> Ensure that you know who you are going to meet and some basic facts about them so that you can start to build rapport as soon as you meet.

The next step is to determine your objectives for the meeting. If you don't have an objective, you will come out of the meeting and the engagement will go nowhere. If you know what your objective is, then you should aim to get to it by the end of the meeting. Some things that you might want to achieve during this meeting might be:

1.  Check that your ideas about their needs are correct.
2.  Develop those needs into ideas that can be sold to them
3.  Understand how the customer makes decisions
4.  Ensure that you can deliver the ideas profitably
5.  Ensure that they can afford to buy it.

While it would be great to come out of the first meeting with an order, it is highly unlikely. So, for any meeting, you should have a fall-back position so that if you are struggling to meet your main objective, you have a lesser objective that you can meet that still helps to move the opportunity forwards.

Another thing to plan is how you are going to present yourself. You have to consider the formality of the meeting, the person that you are meeting and the impression that you want to make. We discussed First Impressions in Chapter 5, Building Trust, so we will not cover that again here. However, it is worth stressing how important making the right first impression is. A few years ago, I moved house and had to get some quotes for the removals. Two people came to give me quotes, one looked like a removal man, took his boots off at the door and used a little notepad to take notes; one came in a sharp suit, kept his shoes on and made all his notes on an iPad. Before I even got the quotes, I knew who I was going to use because the first person demonstrated that he cared about my possessions and wanted to provide a service. The second person clearly did not.

The final part of your preparation is the most important. You must think about the information that you want to learn from the meeting and plan your questions accordingly. Asking questions is the most important skill for a sales person. Most sales people tend to talk too much and listen too little. They are too keen to talk about their product and not understand their customer's needs. If you plan your questions in advance, you have the greatest chance of a successful outcome.

> Asking questions is the most important skill of a sales person.

**Question First**

It is really important that you start the meeting by asking questions. If you start by talking all about your product, then you are likely to talk about things that are not important to the customer. This is a turn off for the customer because they are not interested in things that are not important to them. It is likely that your products do lots of different things and solve lots of different problems. Not all of them will be relevant to every customer.

Asking relevant questions also helps to build trust with your customer. It is clear to them that you have done some research and have a reasonable idea what their work programmes are and what they might need as a result. It demonstrates that you have thought about them as a person rather than as a means to earn a quick sale. Being interested in a person is one of the most effective ways of building trust and asking questions and discussing their responses are great ways to do this.

By asking questions, you find out all of the customer's needs first, often in order of importance. These are the things that they are looking to resolve and if you can help them, they will gladly buy your product. It also enables you to build empathy with the customer and this leads them to be more interested in your products. Once you know their needs, you can focus on the areas of your product that are most applicable to these needs. These will immediately resonate with the customer and gain their attention.

**Questions**

There is a great article in Harvard Business Review called "The Surprising Power of Questions" by Alison Brooks and Leslie John.

Some of the research that it reviews is directly applicable to sales people.

Among the most common complaints people make after having a conversation, such as an interview, a first date, or a work meeting, is "I wish he/she had asked me more questions" or "I can't believe she/he didn't ask me any questions."

Dating back to the 1970s, research suggests that people have conversations in order to exchange information (learning) and form an impression of the other person (liking). Recent research shows that asking questions achieves both.

People who ask many questions are:
- Better liked by their conversation partners;
- Learn more about their partners' interests;
- Are more likely to be able to guess correctly their partners' preferences;
- Are more likely to go on a second date with partners.

> People who ask questions find out more information from their conversation partner and are more liked by them.

The first step in becoming a better questioner is simply to ask more questions. Of course, the number of questions is not the only factor that influences the quality of a conversation. The type, tone, sequence and framing of the questions also matter.

There are four types of questions:
- Introductory questions ("How are you?"),
- Mirror questions ("I'm fine. How are you?"),
- Full-switch questions (ones that change the topic entirely),
- Follow-up questions (ones that solicit more information).

Follow-up questions seem to have a special power. They signal to the other person that you are listening, care and want to know more. People interacting with a person who asks lots of follow-up questions tend to feel respected and heard. In terms of preparation, these questions do not really have to be planned. They should come naturally to the questioner. As a result, when you are planning your questions, you only have to thoroughly plan the opening questions. You should think about what follow up questions might be required but try not to over plan. You want the conversation to flow rather than follow your pre-planned order. We discuss this more later in this chapter when we look at the structure of questions.

In any meeting, whether you have met with the customer before or not, you should be planning your questions to help to build your relationship. Research has shown that the order of questions has a major impact on the relationship and the information received. To build a positive relationship, start with less sensitive questions and build towards more difficult ones.

Imagine you met a stranger and their first question was "What is your biggest regret?" You may be somewhat taken aback and reluctant to answer. However, if you have spent ten minutes building rapport, answering a variety of simple questions about yourself, then the question may not be so harsh and you may be quite happy to answer. So, when looking for find out your customer's biggest needs, do not ask that immediately. Build up to it over the conversation. Start with straight forward questions. If you have done your research well, you should have an idea of what areas they are active in, so ask about those. This helps to demonstrate that you have done your homework and know about the customer. It is also easy for the customer to answer as it is a current project. Only move on to the more difficult questions once you have established yourself.

The questions that we ask must be related to the person that we are asking. I would not ask the head of manufacturing about their payroll needs and I would not ask the head of finance about their assembly line automation needs. These examples are blindingly obvious but for your particular product, think about what would and would not make sense to ask. A poor question can set you back much further than a good question moves you forwards.

Avoid asking a question and then trying to answer it or offer possible answers. This happens all the time in television and radio interviews. The interviewer will ask a question and before anyone can answer, they will have offered their idea of the answer. This closes down the potential answers that you will receive. It biases the person answering towards your preferred answer. Ask the question and then wait for the answer. You will get much more information that way.

**Questioning Structure**

When questioning a customer, it helps to have a structure to your questioning. At the start, you want to be fairly general. As you move on, you can get more specific about the area you are talking about. Try to understand everything you can about a particular topic before you move on to the next. This helps both you and the customer as you can stay focussed on that topic rather than switching between topics which can be confusing and tends to lead to missing information.

Imagine your questions form a funnel. At the top, when you ask your opening question, the answer could come from a wide range of possible answers. When your client does answer, pick one element of their answer and try to understand everything you can about that answer before you move on to the next. As you question more, the scope of each answer will get narrower, like you are moving down through the funnel.

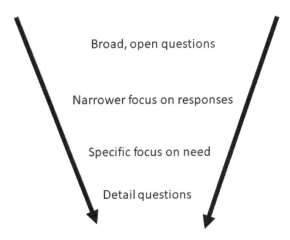

Figure 12.1: The Question Funnel

For example, a sales person selling HR (Human resources/ personnel) software may ask a Head of HR questions like this:

> Sales: "Please can you tell me how your department is organised?"

HR: "We have three groups of people, looking after training and development; compensation and recruitment."

Sales: "Tell me more about compensation, what are their responsibilities?"

HR: "Compensation covers everything to do with what we pay our staff so benefits, payroll, salary benchmarking, bonus plans and share options."

Sales: "That's a very important group then; do you do all of the work yourselves or do you outsource some of it?"

HR: "Yes, we do everything ourselves but we are looking for ways to simplify our processes as we are finding that this is taking more and more time."

Sales: "Are there any particular processes that are taking longer than you would like?"

HR: "Payroll is definitely one of them as it is getting so complicated to keep track of tax changes and legislation as well as all of the different payments that we make to each of the staff."

Sales: "So how long does it take to run each payment period?"

HR: "It is averaging 3-4 days each month."

This is obviously a very simplified conversation but as it progresses, we moved from the whole department, to compensation, to payroll, narrowing the scope each time. We discovered their pain points and the time that it takes to complete the activity each month. From here we can question HR more about the specifics of the different needs and get all of the information that we require to fully understand them. At this point, you can then start talking about your product and how it addresses each of their main needs.

We can group our questions into three categories:

Probing Questions. These are general type questions, aimed at getting a broad view of the work that a company is doing that provides more information than is publicly available. They are the first questions that we ask during the conversation. For example, "please can you tell me how your department is organised?"

Confirmation and Clarification Questions. As we start to learn more about an issue, we have to get specific information about how the issue impacts the client. We have to continue to ask these more direct questions until we understand everything that we want to know about the customer's needs. For example, "How long does it take to run each payment period?"

Solution Questions. These questions start to find out if our proposed solution is likely to be suitable for the customer. There may be some specific requirements for your product that you have to ensure the customer is happy about. For example, if your product operates in the cloud only, you will have to ask about their policy regarding cloud products.

**Types of Question**

There are lots of types of questions but for our purposes, there are only two; open questions and closed questions.

Open Questions. These questions start with

- Who...
- When...
- Where...
- What...
- Why...
- How...

They invite the recipient to talk and to provide information.

Closed Questions. These are the direct opposite. They almost prevent the recipient from talking as they can be answered with a "yes" or a "no".

If you ask a closed question, it is quite possible that the person you are asking will give you a longer answer than just "yes" or "no" but even if they do, the response is likely to be more limited than if you asked an open question.

Asking an open question that invites the person you are asking to give an opinion will elicit much more information than any other type of question. You must start your questioning with open questions. As you move through the dialogue, you may ask more closed questions.

> You will learn much more from a meeting by asking open, opinionated questions.

Beyond this, you may want to consider questions such as:

- What did you mean exactly?
- Tell me more about…
- What happened after that?
- What are the implications in the future?
- Can you give me an example of…

Finally, end by asking "Is there anything else you think that I should know?" This is a really important question as there may be things that you have not thought about. This gives the customer the opportunity to tell you about them. I have asked this question in the past and been told "Yes, I'm leaving the company next week!" This is not likely to be something that you would plan to ask but it is definitely information that you want to know!

**Practise**

Asking questions is a difficult thing to write about in a book. It is something that you have to do more of in order to get better at it. You can practise with anyone. You can set up role plays during work to practise a particular scenario or an important meeting that you have scheduled. You can practice with friends and family by asking questions or playing games. Here are some examples of games or scenarios that you can use to help to improve your questioning techniques.

Game One – asking questions

This is to be done in a group. Randomly assign people to either "high" or "low" groups, preferably without everyone else knowing who is in which group. Pair people up and then get them to have a conversation where, in their pairs, they will either ask lots of questions (high) or few questions (low). Do this a few times so that people get used to it and that it becomes a bit more natural. At the end, see how everyone feels about both the volume of questions they asked and how they felt during each conversation.

Game Two – yes/ no game

The aim of this game is to force your opponent to answer a question with "yes" or "no". You have a minute to ask them as many questions as possible which they have to answer without hesitation (no "ums" or "errs") and without saying "yes" or "no". To be successful, you have to ask a lot of closed questions, where the answer is naturally yes or no. Your opponent will have to think of lots of different ways of answering without saying "yes" or "no". This is generally difficult for the person asking the questions as they have to ask lots of questions with little information to use when formulating the next question.

Game Three – questions only

This is a game from "Whose line is it anyway?" and is an improvisation game. In it, you can only speak in questions so every question has to be answered with another question. You cannot make a statement followed by a question; every sentence has to be a question. You can do this in teams but only two people are involved at any time. If someone fails to ask a question or cannot ask a question, they pass to the next person. You have to have an idea of a scenario to work within to provide some context. An example might be "You are waiting in the reception of a major client and your opposite number from your competitor comes in."

You can watch an example of this game here, *https://www.youtube.com/watch?v=gJqV0UVEoAE*

Game Four – connections

In this game, you have five minutes to discover an interesting, surprising and separate connection you share with each person in your team. (A different connection with each person, not a single connection that every team member shares.)

'Interesting and surprising' does not include working for the same company, living in the same town or country or having the same colour hair. Try to find a connection or something in common that surprises both of you. Discussions can be in pairs or threes and once you have found one, you move onto the next pair. This requires asking questions of each other to discover different facts and using different questions in each pair.

Developing your skill in questioning your customer is probably one of the most important things that a sales person can do to improve their performance. Not only will you find more about their needs but you will lead your customer towards the best solution – your solution – making the resulting sale that much easier to close.

# 13

## ACTIVE LISTENING

*"The word 'listen' contains the same letters as the word 'silent'."*
Alfred Brendel

If we are going to ask our customers some questions, then it stands to reason that we want to listen to the answers. As the saying goes, there's a good reason why we have two ears and one mouth. In sales meetings, we should be listening twice as much as we are speaking, if not more. There's no point asking great questions if we then don't listen to the answers. Listening is itself a skill and we must practise it. However, there are some general things that you should be aware of before you start to practise.

> There is no point asking great questions if we do not listen to the answers.

Listening is not the same as hearing! Our brains are extremely clever at filtering noise and we can tune out background noise and not notice it. We may hear it but we do not listen to it. As the saying goes, there are none so deaf as those that refuse to hear! Listening requires us to actively want to hear what is being said. Our individual biases and ideas sometimes mean that we hear the information that we want to hear but ignore information that we do not want to hear. When we are talking to our customer, we want to ensure that we hear everything, whether we like what is being said or not.

Research suggests that we remember between 25% and 50% of what we hear. During a meeting therefore, we have to improve this so that we take in as much information as possible. We typically do this by making notes. However, it is quite hard to write as fast as someone is talking so we may not be able to write down everything.

On top of all of this, about 60% of our communication is non-verbal. This means that when we are sitting in a meeting, the tone and expression of the speaker is as important as the words that they are saying. We can tell how interested someone is by their tone of voice, which can inform us of how important this subject is to the speaker. This is why meeting people face to face is so important. On the phone, we are missing out on all of this communication. If you know someone well, this is less important but if you really want to make the most of your time with your customer, meeting them in person is really important.

**Hearing is through ears, but listening is through the mind**

Active listening is where you make a conscious effort to hear not only the words that another person is saying but, more importantly, try to understand the complete message being sent. You also want the person speaking to know that you are listening and that they are not just talking to themselves. This can be hard work. Our brains have a tendency to wander and extraneous thoughts will pop in and out of them. This is why we have to practise active listening. It is not something that we can just do.

In order to understand what someone is telling you, you must pay attention to them very carefully. You cannot:

- Allow yourself to become distracted by whatever else may be going on around you;
- Spend time forming counter arguments in your head;
- Look at the pictures on the wall, no matter how interesting they may be;
- Lose track of what the other person is saying.

To enhance your listening skills, you have to let the other person know that you are listening to what he or she is saying. To understand the importance of this, ask yourself if you've ever been engaged in a conversation when you wondered if the other person was listening to what you were saying. You wonder if your message is getting across, or if it's even worthwhile continuing to speak. It feels like talking to a brick wall and it is something you want to avoid.

> Listening involves hearing what is being said and understanding its meaning.

Acknowledgement can be something as simple as a nod of the head or a simple "uh huh." You are not necessarily agreeing with the person, you are simply indicating that you are listening. Using body language, and other signs to acknowledge you are listening, also reminds you to pay attention and not let your mind wander.

You should also try to respond to the speaker in a way that will encourage them to continue speaking, so that you can get the information you require. While nodding and "uh huhing" says you are interested, an occasional question or comment to recap what has been said, communicates that you understand the message as well.

**Pay Attention**

Give the speaker your undivided attention, and acknowledge the message. Recognize that non-verbal communication also "speaks" loudly.

- Look at the speaker directly;
- Put aside distracting thoughts;
- Do not think of an answer;
- Avoid being distracted by environmental factors such as side conversations;
- "Listen" to the speaker's body language.

**Show that you are listening**

Use your own body language and gestures to convey your attention. These should come naturally; if you are having to force them, they may come across poorly. If you are talking to your partner, you will do this anyway, so think about how you do that and repeat it.

- Maintain eye contact;
- Nod occasionally;
- Smile and use other facial expressions;
- Note your posture and make sure it is open and inviting;
- Mirror the speaker;
- Encourage the speaker to continue with small verbal comments;
- Try not to fidget.

**Provide feedback**

Our personal filters, assumptions, judgments and beliefs can distort what we hear. As a listener, your role is to understand what is being said. This may require you to reflect what is being said and ask questions.

- Reflect what has been said by paraphrasing. "What I'm hearing is," and "Sounds like you are saying," are great ways to reflect back.
- Ask questions to clarify certain points. "What do you mean when you say…." or "Is this what you mean?"
- Summarize the speaker's comments periodically.

**Try not to interrupt**

Our brains can process words much faster than anyone can talk and tend to anticipate the ends of sentences before the speaker has got there. As a result, as someone is speaking, our brains are processing the information and developing a response before they have finished their sentence. We therefore have a tendency to interrupt, to add our own opinion to that of the speaker. However, it can be counterproductive. Interrupting does demonstrate that you are paying attention but is irritating for the speaker.

- Try to let the speaker finish each point before asking questions;
- Give them time to think – let them pause without feeling the need to respond;
- Pauses may allow for an interruption but use them to provide feedback.

**Respond appropriately**

Active listening is a model for respect and understanding. You are gaining information and perspective to let you do your job better.

- Summarise what you have just heard;
- Provide any information that is requested;
- Be open and honest in your response;

- Be careful expressing opinions;
- Use facts rather than speculation.

Jack Zenger and Joseph Folkman summarise this in a great paper in Harvard Business Review called "What Great Listeners Actually Do". The conclusions of their study were that:

- The best listeners are those who did not sit silently but who also ask questions that promote discovery and insight such that there was more of a two way dialogue rather than a monologue.

- The best listeners made the conversation a positive experience for the other person such that they felt that that they could say or discuss anything.

- The interaction was seen as a cooperative conversation in which both sides provided feedback and neither became defensive about comments made by the other.

- The best listeners provided positive feedback that is acceptable to the other party and might make them think of different solutions.

In this way, the interaction becomes more of a conversation than a question and answer session. By creating a safe environment, avoiding distractions, focussing on the other person and asking clarification questions, you can have a much more useful interaction rather than just rattling off your rehearsed questions.

**Practise**

As I have said, reading about how to listen, whilst helpful, does not really teach you how to do it. You have to practise, practise and practise again in order to get good at it. Try watching some short videos on YouTube and listening to the whole video without letting your mind wander. These are some good videos about active listening and exercises you can do that improve your listening skills.

*https://www.youtube.com/watch?v=D6-MIeRr1e8*
*https://www.youtube.com/watch?v=ybUJ3-KUlOc*
*https://www.youtube.com/watch?v=-BdbiZcNBXg*
*https://www.youtube.com/watch?v=IwWj_SfDpzg*

They are all about 5 minutes long and will reinforce what you have read in this chapter in a more entertaining way. If you can watch them all the way through without your mind wandering, you are starting to do well.

Move on to longer videos such as these TED talks which are about 10-15 minutes long. Try to get through these without being distracted. If you want to, take notes at the same time so that you get better at listening and writing at the same time.

*https://www.ted.com/talks/tony_salvador_the_listening_bias*

*https://www.ted.com/talks/julian_treasure_5_ways_to_listen_better*

*https://www.ted.com/talks/celeste_headlee_10_ways_to_have_a_be tter_conversation*

It is unlikely that in any client meeting you have to listen for longer than that without a break or asking another question.

Your success as a sales person really comes down to your ability to ask good questions and listen to the answers. Reading about it and watching videos are helpful ways of learning about it but you only get really good at it by doing it.

I recommend that any sales manager spends time with their team working on this skill on a regular basis. If your sales manager is not interested in this, try having a conversation with your partner where you practise these skills. I suggest that you tell them that you are going to do this as they may think you are being a bit strange to begin with as it is probably different from your normal conversation. I also suggest that you don't do it all the time; once or twice a week will suffice. Try to question them and listen to the answers such that you understand everything about what they want to tell you.

I cannot stress enough that questioning and listening requires practise, not reading these chapters, to become a great sales person.

# Value

Definition (from Oxford English Dictionary)

1.  (n) Worth, desirability.

2.  (n) Purchasing power, power of a commodity to purchase others.

3.  (n) Numerical measure of a quantity.

# 14

## VALUE SELLING

*"If the package does not say 'New' these days, it better say 'seven cents off'"*
Spencer Klaw

While sales people sell products, customers buy value. This is a very important thing for any sales person to remember. Unless you can define the value of your product to a customer, then they are going to struggle to understand why they should buy it. As the saying goes, "Value is not determined by those who set the price. Value is determined by those who choose to pay it."

> Sales people sell products, customers buy value.

One of the reasons that I started my sales consultancy was my experience in buying a house. We were not really buying a house, we were buying a home. It was going to be where I lived with my wife and children, created memories, welcomed guests into etc. When you first enter a house, you have to see how you can live there, who will have what bedroom, where will the dog sleep, where the furniture will go and much more.

When we went to look around houses, too many estate agents or sellers told us about how they used the house, or described features that we had no interest in. They made no effort to find out what was important to us or to create a picture of how we might live there. We had to do all of that ourselves, which is not always easy.

However, a house is much easier to understand than some technology. Imagine how some executives feel when presented with new technology that they do not understand; when a sales person lists a number of features that mean nothing to them. The executive has to understand how the technology will improve their business. They have to be able to imagine a brighter future that it will bring. They have to understand the value.

**Price versus Value**

Consider the following scenario. You want to buy a pen and I have two pens for you to consider.

1.   I have two pens, one costs £1 and one costs £100; which would you like to buy?

2.   The £1 pen will run out of ink in 6 weeks, the £100 pen will run out in 6 years; which would you like to buy?

3.   When the £1 pen runs out of ink, you will have to throw it away. When the £100 pen does run out, we will send you a refill through the post for free; which would you like to buy?

4.   If you lose the £1 pen, it is gone forever. The £100 pen contains a tracker device so you can never lose it; which would you like to buy?

5.   If you break the £1 pen, it is gone forever. The £100 pen is made of titanium so will never break; which would you like to buy?

6.   The £1 pen is just a pen. However, if you show the £100 pen in any queue, you will automatically get you to the front of any queue; which would you like to buy?

I suspect that at some stage through all of these points, you have decided to buy the £100 pen. Based purely on the information in 1, it is unlikely that you would buy the £100 pen as it costs so much more for "just a pen". However, as more and more features are added, then the £100 is not "just a pen" and its value increases. This demonstrates that the cost is ultimately unimportant. It is the value that we get for that cost that is important.

What constitutes value to one person does not necessarily constitute value to another. A meal for two at a great restaurant that costs £300 might be considered good value by one couple but not by others. One person may be very happy to buy a pair of shoes for £40 when another would never pay that amount. We all have our own perceptions. Just pricing your products 25% cheaper than your competitor does not mean that everyone will always buy your products. There is more to a purchase than just the price.

Value has little to do with price. A corkscrew is much less expensive than the bottles of wine that it will open but it is crucial to the enjoyment of the wine, as anyone who has tried to uncork a bottle without a corkscrew will tell you! Only if a product is a commodity does price really matter. An item can be considered a commodity when it has no other inherent communicable "value" than its price. Plain, white envelopes are a good example – all brands are basically the same and if we are buying them online, we will generally buy the cheapest. However, if we are out shopping for other goods, we may choose to buy the envelopes in the most convenient store, even if they are more expensive than in another store. In this case, there is value in the time saved by buying them with everything else rather than visiting a number of shops to find the cheapest. This can be considered a perceived value in that it is only of value in those specific circumstances.

Creating and selling goods that are a commodity is extremely difficult as there is a lot of competition from large companies. To compete in a market like this, it is necessary to create a perceived value. For example, you might use recyclable packaging; use all renewable energy to create it or manufacture and sell locally. These factors create a "different" product and appeal in ways that the large company cannot. By doing this, you are creating something bigger than you are actually selling and creating value in that way.

**Value Proposition**

Four Doctors each write a proposal:

1. I'm a Doctor.
2. I'm a Doctor. I help people.
3. I'm a Doctor. I help people with cancer.
4. I'm a Doctor. I help people who have cancer that has re-occurred.

John is a middle-aged man who had skin cancer a few years ago and has just been diagnosed with cancer again. He is looking for expert advice and while all of the doctors can help, indeed they may all be equally qualified and experienced, only Doctor number 4 has actually articulated the value that they are bringing to their consultation. It creates a very simple choice for John.

> A good value proposition should define the specific value that your customer will receive from your product related to their specific needs.

Your value proposition tells customers why they should buy your product and not the competitor's. It is important to define and articulate as often as possible. As with many things, there are two versions. A marketing value proposition is generic and should appeal to as broad a cross section of your customers as possible. A sales value proposition is specific to one customer and should define the specific value that they will receive from your products based on their specific needs.

To write a value proposition, you must identify all the benefits your product offers and describe what makes these benefits valuable. If it is a sales value proposition, then it must be related back to the customer's specific needs that have led to your proposal.

A good sales value proposition:

- Is easy to understand by anyone who reads it, even if they do not fully understand your technology;
- Communicates specific results that your customer will get from implementing your product;
- Explains how it is different and better than any competition;
- Can be read and understood quickly.

A value proposition isn't just the product you agree to deliver to the customer. It is not a slogan or a mission statement. It is not a list of features and functions that your product contains. It absolutely must be about the benefits that the product provides with a quantification of the value if at all possible.

**Features versus Benefits**

One of the biggest problems that I find with most sales people is the confusion of features and benefits. This is also one of the most crucial things to get right. Let us start with a definition of both.

**Feature**. A feature is a distinctive characteristic of a product that sets it apart from similar items.

**Benefit**. A desirable attribute of a product, which a customer will receive by using the product.

> A benefit is a statement of how things will be better as a result of the solution provided.

The best way I have found to determine if you have defined a feature or benefit is to ask yourself, "So what?" If I read a statement and I do not understand why I care about it, then the chances are you have written a feature. Only once you can be completely certain that you understand how your customer will be better off, can you state that this is a benefit. I will illustrate this with the following story.

A number of years ago I went to buy a new television. I knew that I had to get a 32" flat screen television but beyond that, I was not sure what I wanted. I had no specific brand in mind nor any other specific features that were important to me. In the shop, there were 8 televisions that matched my criteria; 7 of the televisions were £500, one was £900. Intrigued, I asked the shop assistant why one was so much more expensive than the others.

"Ah, that one has a 100Hz refresh rate, the others are all 50Hz" was the response.

Now, I understood all of the words in that sentence but I did not understand why it should be worth paying so much more for. So, naturally, I asked

"So what?"

"Well, that means that the image on the screen of the 100Hz television refreshes twice as fast as on the screen of the 50Hz ones" was the response. "This means that fast moving action, like sport, will have a much sharper, clearer image."

As it happens, I planned to mostly watch sport on this television so it was a fairly easy decision as to which television I bought. I did not buy a 100Hz refresh rate; I bought a better viewing experience. I did not buy a specific feature; I bought the value that it gave me.

Customers buy value, not features and functions. The problem is that most sales people sell features. Unless those features are translated into value, then the customer will not be able to decide that the product is worth buying. It will not be possible to do this unless you understand what is important to the customer.

> Unless features of a product are translated into value then a customer will not be able to decide that a product is worth buying.

In the example above, the sales assistant had no idea that I wanted to watch sport on the television, they just used that as the example. However, as soon as they said it, it was obvious to me that this was the television I had to buy. Indeed, I completely blew my budget by doing so. My research had told me that all 32" televisions were about £500 so that was what I had expected to spend. However, once I understood the value of the more expensive television, I was happy to buy it.

You should be able to define benefits as one of the following:

- Saves time
- Saves money
- Reduces risk

These are the essential things that any business is trying to do when they deploy new technology. Every benefit statement that you make should be tied to one or other of these.

All benefits have to be as specific to a customer as possible. Imagine a tractor sales person approaching a farmer. It is fairly obvious to anyone that a tractor can plough a field much faster than a horse so surely the farmer would want a tractor? That is a reasonable assumption unless the farmer only wants to plough a few acres and has many other uses for the horse that the tractor simply cannot satisfy. As a sales person, you will only know that by asking the farmer about their farm, further demonstrating why asking questions is so important before trying to sell anything.

To be successful at selling, the sales person must translate the features and functions of their product into specific benefits for their customer. Generic benefits should be reserved for marketing materials. To sell, you have to be specific. If you are unable to state why a feature will benefit a customer then you either have not asked enough questions or the feature is of no value to them.

In general, I only ever include three or four benefits of a product in a sales pitch. If you cannot persuade a customer with the best four reasons, another ten are unlikely to make much of a difference. Too many people continue to list feature after feature in the hope that they will finally find one that makes sense to the customer. If you understand your customer's problems well enough, you should know which benefits are most useful to them.

**Quantifying value**

If you buy solar panels in UK, the sales person is legally obliged to quantify the value to you. The panels provide value by:

1. Reducing the amount of electricity you take from the grid, saving money;
2. Excess electricity is diverted to an immersion heater to provide hot water, saving money;
3. Any further excess electricity is sent into the grid, making you money.

Based on the panels that you are installing and your current electricity usage, it is possible to calculate how much money you can save / earn from the panels and thereby how long it takes for the upfront cost to be recouped. This is a legal requirement of solar panel sales people to avoid customers being ripped off. It is a straight forward calculation so relatively easy to provide. Not all of the benefits of technology can be so easily quantified. I cannot measure how much extra enjoyment I receive from my 100Hz refresh rate television over a 50Hz refresh rate.

Imagine that we have a customer who has a process that produces a widget in 10 hours at a cost of £100. I can provide a new product that reduces this by 10%, saving £10. If my product costs £100, then the customer can be in profit after they have produced 10 widgets, which is good value. However, if my product costs £100,000, then it is going to take a lot longer to make this money back and it may not represent such good value.

This calculation is straight forward for a simple process. However, for a longer, complicated process, it can be hard to quantify the value of a product that impacts just a small part of that process. In this instance, you have to try to break the process down into as small a part as possible and see what value you can quantify. Even then, it may be very difficult to quantify the precise value of a purchase. If you are able to demonstrate previous success with another customer and their process improvement, then that will definitely help.

> You should try to quantify the value of your product to your customer so that it is easier for them to say "yes".

When you focus on the value gained as a result of the purchase, you get the client thinking less about the cost. Cost becomes much less important. I know of companies in the oil industry that charge about £100,000 for a product that can return several million pounds to their customer. In this instance, the cost almost becomes irrelevant. An investment that delivers a 10 times return is not something that any company is likely to turn down.

The converse of this is that the selling organisation can feel like they lose out in this deal. They provide a product that makes millions for their customer but they only get paid a fraction of that amount. It can be very difficult to equate the cost of a product to the value that it delivers. An oil well may cost ten million dollars to drill. It might find an oil field worth four billion dollars or forty billion dollars or it might find nothing at all. The cost of the well has not changed but the derived value can vary enormously. The cost of the well does not reflect any of the risk of the outcome. The oil company is taking all of the risk. The drilling company will get paid regardless of the result.

Tying risk and reward into pricing is very difficult and I am inclined to avoid it. The balance of risk and reward is almost certainly in favour of the purchaser rather than the seller. However, if this is a requirement for a deal, then understanding the risk is absolutely crucial to being able to construct a sensible win-win arrangement.

**Value Selling**

The simple premise for selling is:

1. Customer has a problem which is costing them time/money;
2. You have a product which can solve the problem;
3. If the product costs less than the problem, you can make a sale.

If you cannot demonstrate this, then you are going to struggle. It does not mean that you cannot sell but it will be much more difficult. I have known companies who buy product simply because they believe that they will be useful to them at some stage, not necessarily now. I have known companies buy products because the Managing Director wanted them, regardless of how valuable they are. However, these are the exceptions and you cannot build a career on exceptions.

If you want to be successful, you have to focus on the customers for whom you can provide value and preferably measurable value.

# 15

## WHY CHANGE?

*"If you never change your mind, why have one?"*
Edward de Bono

**Making Decisions**

S tudies have shown that up to 60% of sales opportunities are lost to "no decision" rather than competitors. In these instances, the companies decide to do nothing rather than do something. This may seem strange as they clearly believed at some point that they needed a new product or they had a problem that had to be fixed yet they chose to do nothing about it.

> Up to 60% of sales opportunities are lost to no decision rather than competitors.

The simple fact is that without a compelling case for change, companies will tend to do nothing. Most companies "already have something that does that". For example, if they are in business to manufacture something, then they generally already have the means of production. It may not be big enough or fast enough but it does what is required. I have known companies who will do everything that they possibly can in Excel rather than buy specific software to do that work. Excel had already been purchased so if it can do the job, no matter how difficult it may be or how inefficient it is, then they will use that rather than buy more appropriate software.

Human beings are generally risk averse and do not like change. This applies in business as much as it applies in our personal life, if not more so. If a purchasing decision proves to be incorrect, then someone might be demoted or worse still, lose their job. As a result, people will frequently choose not to make a decision for fear of making the wrong decision. Buying new equipment or implementing a new technology comes with risk. There may be a loss in productivity at the start as people get used to the new processes. If things do not go to plan, then improvements may not happen. All of these fears inhibit decisions to buy.

As a result, a customer has to understand the opposite view. What is the risk of doing nothing? How much better will life be if they do decide to proceed? Without a clear understanding of the risk of doing nothing or a compelling vision of "what better looks like," customers will tend to do nothing. Imagine if they do not implement a time saving process and they lose customers and have to make cutbacks to survive. This is not something that any business wants so the risk of not proceeding can be higher than the risk of implementing the new process.

> Without a clear vision of "what better looks like", customers will tend to do nothing.

To be successful in selling, particularly for improvements or replacements, sales people have to first persuade the customer to change before they can persuade them to buy their product. Of course, in almost any market place, there is a choice of products that can do the same thing. This leads to a further complication. Having too much choice can also lead to a customer doing nothing.

**The Paradox of Choice**

If you look at a certain online supermarket, there are over 100 different products labelled "salad dressing"! With all that choice, it is difficult for anyone to decide which one to buy. Salad dressing is essentially very simple – it is mostly oil and vinegar, possibly some lemon juice or honey, some herbs and garlic. Consequently, as there are so many different combinations of ingredients, there are lots of different products.

When browsing the site, it is possible to review all the ingredients, check the dietary information and read reviews that previous buyers have posted. However, with over 100 to review, who is likely to spend lots of time reviewing each one before making a decision? The chances are that they simply going to buy the one that they bought last time, assuming that they liked it. There is no compelling reason to change; there is no risk to staying with the same product. As a result, people tend to buy the same thing all the time and all that choice is wasted on them.

Research has shown that too many choices can make us unhappy and sometimes lead to no decision at all. As the number of options increases, the costs, in terms of the time and effort to gather the information required to make a good choice, also increase. Even if they make a choice, people will be less certain that they have made the right choice and indeed they anticipate that they will regret their choice. All of this leads to worry and persuades people not to change.

Again, this is equally applicable in a business. Getting decisions wrong can lead to business failure and job losses which are not good for anyone. However, there is a way to limit these problems and increase your chances of success in selling.

## Who wants to change?

Studies have shown that, at any one time, only about half of all possible customers, are close to making a decision to buy something. The other half are quite happy with what they have. These numbers are in respect of your product, not across the entire business.

Consider your personal life. Every week, more likely than not, you will go to the supermarket to buy food. However, you will probably go to the shoe shop to buy shoes much less regularly. So, if you are a shoe sales person, then you cannot expect to see the same customer all the time. They will come at the point where they decide to buy new shoes.

We can divide the buying cycle into three stages.

1. Status quo – customers are very happy with what they have. There is about a 1% chance of them deciding to buy your product. This represents about 50% of your potential customers.
2. Window of Dissatisfaction – customers start to begin to be unhappy. If you introduce your customer to your product at this stage, before they have decided to do anything, then you have about a 75% chance of them buying your product. This represents about 40% of your potential customers.

3. Searching for alternatives – customers have to do something to resolve their problem. At this stage, the customer is likely to come to you but also go to all of your competitors. As a result, they are less likely to buy your product; indeed, there is only a 17% chance of them buying. This represents about 10% of your potential customers.

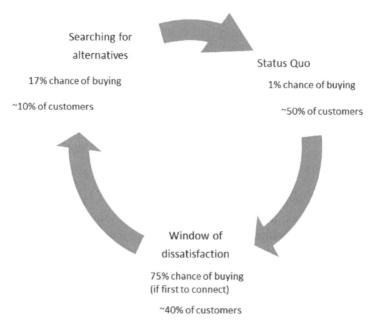

Searching for
alternatives

17% chance of buying

~10% of customers

Status Quo

1% chance of buying

~50% of customers

Window of
dissatisfaction

75% chance of buying
(if first to connect)

~40% of customers

Figure 15.1: The Buying Cycle

Think about this in terms of shoes. For most of the time, we have sufficient pairs and we are quite happy with them – we are at status quo. However, over time, they may become worn or tatty; alternatively, we may have an important event on the horizon that requires a new pair. This is when we enter the window of dissatisfaction. We may walk past a shoe shop and, on the spur of the moment, go in to buy a new pair. This is quite likely to be the first shoe shop that we walk past and if we find a pair that we like, we will probably buy them. However, if that does not happen, then eventually our shoes will be too worn or tatty to wear or our important event is tomorrow and we will be forced to go shopping. We are then searching for alternatives and may go to four or five shops before we finally decide on a pair.

> Our best chance of making a sale is with customers who are just getting to be unhappy with what they are doing.

Based on this, it is quite obvious that our best chance of making a sale is with a customer who is in the window of dissatisfaction. 40% of customers are in that position and if we are the first person to try to help them, three out of four customers will buy from us. Those are great odds! Of course, no one advertises the fact that they are unhappy with what they have. It is up to us to work that out. This is why our customer research and needs analysis are so important. We are trying to identify those companies that are in the window of dissatisfaction.

Lots of people will say that sales people are lucky to show up at the right time. To an extent, that is true as you can never be totally sure when a customer will leave the status quo. Turning up just as they enter the window of dissatisfaction gives the greatest chance of winning a deal. However, for most sales people, it is hard work and good research that allows them to turn up at the right time.

The other way to go about this is to find customers who are in status quo, who are happy with their current situation, and then push them into the window of dissatisfaction. This achieves two things; it gets more customers into the window of dissatisfaction and also means that you are the first person to help them and so are the most likely to win any deal that comes out of it. Unfortunately, buyers are aware of this! I have seen presentations to buyers that stated "Remember that sales and marketing professionals are trained to disrupt your confidence in the status quo". However, this should not stop us trying!

To achieve this, we have to persuade our customers to change. We do not want to talk about our own product, we just want to persuade them that all is not well and that they have to change. If we can do that, then we are in a great position to be successful.

> If we can persuade our customer to change their processes, then we have a greater chance of persuading them to buy our product.

Many years ago, I worked for a software company that was trying to break into a particular market. To do that, we had to persuade the dominant customer in that market to use our software. For a variety of reasons, this was considered almost impossible, until we did! However, the reason that drove them to switch was that they wanted their scientists to change their workflows dramatically and the only way that they could do this was by changing the software that they used. They knew that if they kept the same software, users would revert back to their old workflows and nothing would change. To make the workflow changes effective, they had to change their software and they chose to change to us. We would never have won until the customer decided to change.

**Logic vs Emotion**

On a personal level, we quite often buy things that we do not need; another pair of shoes, a chocolate bar or the latest video game. We do not need them; we just want them. We may buy them on a whim, based on our emotions at the time. We generally do not spend a long time deciding what to buy or debating whether the cost is worth it. We do not look at all the different options, we just buy the one that we like the look of. These purchases are very much governed by emotion, with very little logic applied.

When we make a major purchase, such as a house, a car or even a vacuum cleaner, we generally make a more considered purchase. We consider our options, we look at the different features and functions of the item, before we decide which particular product to buy. However, there is still a degree of emotion applied to the decision.

A house is generally the most expensive thing that any of us will ever buy for ourselves. Before we go and look at a house, we decide on some basic parameters. How many bedrooms do we need? Where abouts do we want to live? Do we want a garden? Consultants that help people when they are buying a new home will have up to one hundred features of a new house that they will ask buyers to consider. However, once we have decided on all of these features and we have a short list of houses to view, the final decision quite often comes down to emotion and how much we like a house within the first few minutes of walking through the door.

> Emotion and logic both contribute to our decision about whether to buy and what to buy.

So, emotion and logic both have their part to play in deciding whether to buy and what to buy. Logic informs our decision about whether to buy. Do we need a bigger house? Can we afford a bigger house? However, emotion informs our decision about which one to buy. This is exactly the same in business. Even though it is a business that does the buying, it is people within that business that make the decisions about what to buy.

Happiness is an emotion so it stands to reason that unhappiness is an emotion. If we are unhappy about something, we try to fix it to make us happy again. If our car keeps breaking down and causing us to be late, we will probably be unhappy. Our solution is possibly to buy a more reliable car. In business, if a process is poor or results are disappointing, we may be unhappy and want to fix things. This frequently leads to a business buying a product to help.

In the status quo position, the business is happy. If we, as sales people, push them out of the that position, into the window of dissatisfaction, we make them unhappy and those emotions will drive a purchasing decision. So, how can we cause this to happen?

**Why do we change?**

Can you remember the last time that you changed your mind about something significant? As we get older, we tend to become more conservative and change less. It takes a lot to change our mind, despite the fact that the results are often much better than staying as we are. We talk about being forced to change as being pushed out of our comfort zone. It may be as simple as trying a new cuisine, going to a new country or bungee jumping over the Zambezi River. However, the results are generally positive.

1.  You get to experience more;
2.  You get to find out what you are really capable of;
3.  You become more flexible and adaptable;
4.  You frequently have more fun.

Even if you do not ultimately enjoy it, you at least have a great story to tell!

In the business world, there has to be more rational, less thrill-seeking reasons to change. However, there are still plenty of reasons for change. You just have the find the right one for each customer. In many respects, these reasons are the very things that we have to use to initiate our interaction with our customers, as we discussed in Chapter 9, How to get through the front door.

**Technology**. Technology has let us do things faster and cheaper and will continue to do so. Word processors enabled us to create printed documents quicker; laptops enable us to create documents on the move; smart phones enable us to view those documents anywhere with a phone signal. Selling technology that reduces costs and improves productivity really should be straight forward as long as we focus on the results rather than the technology itself.

**Customer Needs**. Change is happening all around us and as a result, the requirements and use of any product will change over time. This will create demands for new types of products and open up new areas of opportunity for companies to meet those needs. These are the sorts of things that a business should be looking for as a matter of course but frequently, they are too focussed on running the business to notice. If you find some research or insights that show how companies are changing, then this is a useful way to persuade your customer to change.

**The Economy**. The economy is something that a business has little control over and frequently just has to react to. I am writing this book in the middle of the Covid-19 pandemic, possibly the biggest disrupter of the economy in our lifetime. Changes to the economy will change the way that a business works in both positive and negative ways and both can be stressful. This will push a business into the window of dissatisfaction without much input from a sales person. In this instance, the sales person must be ready to react and reach out to the business as soon as things start to change.

**Competition**. Competition is the bedrock of capitalism. However, companies can often get comfortable with each other and the need for change gets diminished. The entrance of a new competitor or a change in how one company works can often disrupt the status quo and force change as a result. Again, if a sales person can bring new insights to a business about how others are working, then this will generally be well received and enable them to win new sales.

**Government Regulations**. This is possibly one of the biggest drivers for change. Regulations generally come with penalties for non-compliance. Some health and safety regulations can have unlimited fines for failing to comply. No company can afford to fail to meet them, both from a financial and a reputational perspective. If you can help a company to better comply with regulations, then you have a great way of persuading them to change. This applies even more if they are new regulations or often forgotten about regulations. Small businesses in particular struggle with these as they do not have enough staff to keep track of everything like this. If you help companies to stay compliant, you have a great way of persuading them to change.

Once you have moved a customer from their happy status quo position into the window of dissatisfaction, you have a great opportunity to persuade them to buy your product that helps them return to the status quo. However, just making them unhappy is not sufficient. They must be convinced that if they do change, that they will be happier as a result, that they will make more money or that they will be fully compliant. You have to get them to see an image of what "better" looks like.

**Case Studies**

It is only by seeing what "better" looks like that a customer can be persuaded to change. Just being unhappy is not sufficient. In our personal lives, we see other people with new, fashionable clothes and think "I'll be happier / have more friends / attract more attention if I wear those clothes". We adopt a new wardrobe to change our appearance because we see other people wearing similar things and see how that has impacted their life. It is almost impossible to get us to change our wardrobe to clothes that no one else is wearing. We require the reassurance of seeing other first. To persuade our customers to change, we have to show them how others are being successful by having changed.

Case studies show your prospective customer how other companies have changed their business and been successful. They feature real world situations and are written from the perspective of the customer rather than the product provider. This is very important as you want your customer to experience the transition and they can only do this by seeing it from their own perspective.

> Case studies show your prospective customer how their business can change and be successful.

Generic case studies can serve a useful purpose but the best ones are those that are based on problems very similar to those that your customer is facing. This means that you have to have many of them, to match as many as possible of the problems that you solve and the products that you provide.

A good case study is set out much like a good proposal.

The objectives – what was the company trying to achieve?

The needs – what was stopping them from achieving those objectives?

The features – what product did you provide that helped them?

The benefits – how was the company better off as a result?

If you are able to quantify the benefits, it will be a much more powerful case study as a result. A 10% increase in revenue is much more enticing than simply stating that the customer was able to increase revenues as a result of the changes.

Of course, you will have to get the approval of your customer to produce a case study document with facts and figures. Quite often they are happy to participate because it demonstrates to their customers how good they are. However, it is possible that they will not agree. In this case, you require a different way to present the information. You may simply be able to anonymise the document but it may be necessary to just tell the story of the success.

A verbal story can often be just as powerful as a written document. As we have discussed, the way that we tell a story leads it to be more memorable than something that is read. You can include much more emotion in a verbal story than you ever can in a written story. You can also be sure that your client is fully conversant with the story rather than just leaving them a document that they may never get around to reading. This should give them the confidence that change is for the better.

# 16

## WHY ARE YOU UNIQUE?

*"What sets you apart can sometimes feel like a burden and it's not. And a lot of the time, it's what makes you great."*

Emma Stone

Having established that the customer wants to change, we now have to persuade them that they must choose you. As we stated in the previous chapter, if you are the person to persuade a company to change, you are in pole position to sell them your product. However, even then, companies may want to shop around or they may already be looking for alternatives by the time that you talk to them. It is unusual for you to be the only possible option for them to choose. As a result, you may have to persuade your customer to choose your product rather than the competition. To do that, you have to focus on the uniqueness of what you offer.

**Competition**

We all have competition. It is very unusual for there to be a single supplier of a particular product. Indeed, Competition Authorities work very hard to ensure that there is competition in all walks of life.

Consider the range of smart phones available in the shops today. They come from Apple, Samsung, Huawei, Google, Sony, Nokia etc. In essence, they all do the same things – make calls, send texts, take pictures, browse the internet. However, there are subtle differences between them that make us select one rather than the other.

If you take any group of people and ask them why they bought the particular phone that they have, they will almost certainly give you different reasons. I use an iPhone mostly because I cannot be bothered to learn how to use a new operating system and phone. However, others will pick phones because of the camera, integration with other devices, network provider etc. We may have picked the same phone but for different reasons. It all depends on what is important to us and that varies from one person to another.

In the same way, our customers have a choice and can choose us or our competition. It is therefore really important that you understand why they would choose you.

**You versus the Competition**

No product is completely unique. There will always be aspects of your product that are very similar to others and aspects that are not. Consider the Venn diagram below:

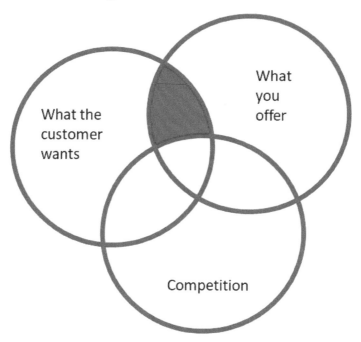

Figure 16.1: Why are you unique?

The three circles represent the functionality that:
1.  Your customer wants
2.  You offer
3.  Your competition offers.

The diagram is not drawn to scale! Hopefully there is a greater overlap between 1 and 2 than I have drawn!

There is obviously functionality that you both offer that is of no interest to the customer and functionality that you both offer that matches what the customer wants. There will also be some functionality that the customer wants that neither of you can offer.

The critical area is marked in red. This is the functionality that the customer wants and that only you can offer. Ultimately, it will be this that wins you a competitive deal. This is functionality that only you can offer. This must be more important to the customer than the functionality that the competition can offer but you cannot.

> Your customer will pick your solution because of its unique features that are important to them.

To be successful, you have to stress the functionality where you are strongest and down play the functionality that you lack.

In most cases, there will be a variety of functionalities that are unique, either in what they do or how they do it. They may only be subtle differences but they can cause a big difference in the perception of your product. It is important to have an overall view of the differences between your product and the competition as it relates to each opportunity. This can be done using a form of Boston Square, relating uniqueness to value.

For each element of your offering, you must define how unique it is to your product and how valuable it is to the customer. You can then plot the results on a diagram like the one below.

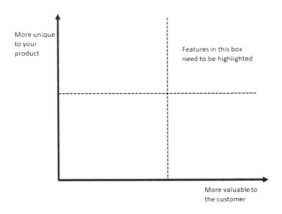

Figure 16.2: Relating value and uniqueness

The features and functions that appear in the top right-hand box have to be ones that you focus on. These are most unique to your product and most valuable to the customer. For items in the bottom right-hand box, you have to find ways to either improve them (now or a promise to improve in the future) or minimise their impact.

Items on the left-hand side are not so important to the customer so less attention has to be paid to these. The bottom left-hand side should barely be mentioned, they are neither unique to you nor important to the customer. Features and functions in the top left-hand side can be explored some more by asking questions of the customer. Find out why they are not important to them. The customer may never have thought about them so you may find a way to move them to the right-hand side of the chart. If not, do not talk about them too much as they can distract the customer from the things that they consider to be most important.

Bear in mind that your competition will be doing the same thing. So, to do this analysis effectively, you will also have to know where your competition is strong. This can be quite difficult to find out in some cases but the more that you can discover about them, the better you can position your product as the best one.

**Uniqueness**

There are a variety of ways of defining uniqueness.

1. If only one single example of a thing exists. For example, the Rosetta Stone and the Mona Lisa are unique, one of a kind, objects.

2. Something is unique if it is limited by situation or geography. For example, kangaroos are unique to Australia.

3. A situation may have a unique outcome. For example, an equation may have only one solution which makes that solution unique.

4. Uniqueness may just be unusual or having no equal. For example, someone may have a unique smile or a unique skill that is unmatched.

With technology, it can be very difficult to be completely unique. If something is unique, then its uniqueness generally does not last very long! There are always other ways of completing a task, possibly slower or clumsier, but there are alternatives. Unique features are not always clear cut and sometimes they may just be the perception of the customer rather than fact. To be successful in differentiating your product, you have to be able to highlight just some aspects that are unique rather than focussing on the whole product.

Once you have understood what is unique about your product and how it relates to your customer, you should consider reviewing your definition of a good customer, as originally defined in Chapter 8, What does a good customer look like? Unique features of your product that are important to a particular type of customer should make those customers more important to you than other customers.

**What else is unique?**

Do not limit your analysis to just the product that you are selling. There are other aspects of your offer to your customer that could be unique. For example:

1. Support. You may provide 24x7 support or have offices in all locations where your customer is located.

2. You may offer a different pricing model that is more appealing to your customer.

3. You may deliver the technology via a different process that is more helpful to your customer.

4. You may provide product updates on a faster turnaround that your competitor.

All of these are ways of differentiating yourself from your competition. With many technologies, the differences in the technology may not be great so you have to find other ways of being unique.

One final element of uniqueness to consider is your relationship with the customer. While this is not related to your product, it can have a bearing on the decision that the customer makes. If you have become a trusted advisor, then that relationship will make a difference to how your customer views your product. If there are areas of doubt, then any promise that you make to eliminate those doubts will help to remove them. If there is little trust, then any promise that you make will be ineffective. This is why trust is so important, especially when there are only a few small differences between your product and the competition.

**Non-uniqueness**

This is one of the things that frustrates me the most. Far too many companies use non-unique descriptions of their products to advertise themselves or their products. I once came across a banner for a further education college. On it, they included the statement "We have a passion for learning and skills". Can you possibly imagine a further education college that is not interested in learning? That is their sole purpose. Do they really think that they are differentiating themselves by stating this?

In a similar way, many technology companies promote their support or customer care as being great as though that was unique. I doubt that there are many technology companies still in business these days that do not have good customer support. Every company claims to have this, so you are not really differentiating yourself by claiming to have it.

To be unique, you have to do something or offer something that no one else offers. This can be difficult to define and does require quite a lot of thought. Using stock lists of functionality or features is not the way to go about it. You have to look at things from the perspective of the customer.

**Why does your customer care?**

Ultimately, if the things that make your product unique are not important to your customer, they will not matter. Every customer is different and what is unique and useful to one will not necessarily be unique and useful to another. This means that you must have as long a list of uniquenesses as possible. You also must have an idea of why they are important to your customer. Again, this will vary from customer to customer but a generic understanding is a good starting point.

Customers care about features that make them more efficient or reduce the risk of accidents happening. They care about making more money or reducing their overheads. You must be able to translate the unique features into value for the customer, as discussed in Chapter 14, Value Selling.

# 17

## WHAT DOES A GOOD OPPORTUNITY LOOK LIKE?

*"The reason a lot of people do not recognize opportunity is because it usually goes around wearing overalls looking like hard work."*

Thomas Edison

E very sales person that I know has spent time chasing after a sale that never happened. Sales people are frequently very competitive and will spend time chasing all opportunities hoping to win them all. That can result in a lot of wasted time and effort that could have been better spent elsewhere. In the same way that not every customer is a good customer today, not every opportunity is worth pursuing.

Creating opportunities is easy. If you have a product that works, you might convince yourself that every company is a potential customer and therefore an opportunity. Clearly, that is not the case and many such "opportunities" can be eliminated with a quick analysis of each customer. However, even within your best customers, there will be a range of opportunities and usually too many to chase all at the same time. With so many opportunities, it can be difficult to identify the ones that are most likely to close and therefore most worthy of your attention. If you can achieve a higher rate of closing by working smarter, then you should be more successful overall.

> By focussing on the best opportunities, you are more likely to be successful and make more money.

**Opportunity Identification.**

Ken Tencer, CEO SpyderWorks is quoted as saying "A good opportunity is one that is relevant. To know which ones are most relevant, you have to be able to assess them against pre-determined criteria."

A number of years ago, my son and I had accumulated lots of things that we didn't want. He had grown out of his baby toys, I had household goods that I didn't want. So, I decided that we would take them to a car boot sale. I thought that we could raise some money, have a day out and he could learn about selling and dealing with people.

For us, the goods that we had to sell were not worth anything; we didn't use them, we didn't want them. However, for the people who came along, they were not worthless. They could make use of them and were prepared to spend money to buy them. While we charged a range of prices, we typically charged £1-2 for each item. To us, any sale was a good sale. Cash in our hands was better than having to take the goods home again, even if we did not sell an item for quite as much as we would have liked. As a result, we made about £80 profit and took home very few items. Any sale was a good sale.

Think about why shops have sales. Clothes shops in particular will have sales twice a year. In mid-summer, people have bought the summer clothes that they require and want to start to buy winter clothes. So, the shops discount the summer clothes to generate quick sales and to make space for the winter clothes. The economics of each product line is such that not every item of clothing has to be sold at full price to make the line profitable. So, by that time of year, it is more important to have full price winter clothes in store than unwanted summer clothes. Any sale of the discounted clothes is both profit and more room to sell full price clothes. Any sale is a good sale.

In the business to business world, it is not so easy to just have a sale of cheap goods. We have a limited number of opportunities and must maximise our prices as much as possible. However, not every opportunity is equally important or equally likely to close. A sale to our best customer is more likely to close than a sale to a company that we have never worked with before. A sale of 100 units is more important than a sale of 1 unit. The effort to sell 100 units is typically more than the effort to sell 1 unit but possibly only 2-3 times more; it is certainly not 100 times more. As a result, we have to focus on the more important opportunities.

**Sales Opportunity Management**

The difference between companies that just get by and companies that are very successful is quite often due to sales opportunity management. Sales opportunity management is the process of tracking each potential sale from an initial lead to a closed sale. Not all leads become sales but if all of them are tracked, then you can compare them and focus on the those that are most important and most likely to close.

> Sales opportunity management tracks each lead to a sale. Successful companies will apply this process rigorously.

There are a variety of studies and a variety of statistics covering this area. On average, about 10% of leads become tangible opportunities and about 10% of those become an actual sale. It can take around 100 days to convert an initial lead into a closed sale. This effectively means that you have to have 100 leads to close a sale and each lead takes 100 days to close. Those are large numbers! Clearly, this will vary from product to product – some products that I have sold have required only 3 or 4 leads to close a sale but they may take 6-9 months to close. Whichever way you look at it, anything that you can do to improve these numbers will have a dramatic impact on your overall success.

Other studies show that, on average, it takes 50% longer to lose a deal than to win one. This is because sales people are still chasing an opportunity, when the customer has already decided but has not told the sales person, or that they are desperately trying to "win back" a lost opportunity by refusing to admit defeat. Think about how much more worthwhile it would be to spend that time chasing opportunities that are more likely to close.

In Chapter 8 we reviewed what a good customer looks like. However, even within our best customers, not all opportunities are equal. We have to apply a similar process to ranking our opportunities across all customers to chase the most important ones first.

**Identifying Good Opportunities**

There are a number of ways that we can go about identifying a good opportunity,

**Experience**. Experience is extremely useful. It teaches us so much and we can eliminate opportunities based on what we have done before, what we have won and lost in the past. The problem with this though is that it tends to be very personal, my experience will tell me that an opportunity isn't great but that doesn't really help anyone else unless we consider peer reviews.

Peer reviews are used by many industries. Technical papers have to be peer reviewed before they are published; it is common for one group of people in an organisation to review the work of a similar group and to offer advice as to how they might improve. Peer reviewing opportunities takes advantage of other people's experiences and is a great way of assessing whether opportunities are worth pursuing.

**History**. History is similar to experience but is more based on actual data. Sales opportunities can be tracked in a CRM system with customer contacts and activities. It may be possible to use this data to determine which activities were effective and which were not. It may be possible to find relationships between closed deals and other factors.

I think that this works more effectively in business to consumer sales where there are many customers and many customer contacts that are automatically tracked through a CRM system. By analysing clicks or open rates of emails, it is possible to determine what works and what does not and increased sales can come about by working more with the things that work. However, in many business to business relationships, there are far fewer contacts and little automation so this is more difficult to do.

**Feedback**. Feedback is an extremely useful way of learning lessons. In sales, we have a tendency to only look for feedback once we have lost an opportunity but it is equally valid to ask for feedback once you have won. Ask your customer for feedback at the end of every opportunity, whether it is won or lost.

Feedback questions can include:
- What factors most impacted your decision?
- Why did you choose a competitor?
- What stopped you from buying from us?
- Was anything missing that would have changed your mind?

Once you learn new information, ensure that you act upon it to reduce the chance of it happening again. It is amazing how many people working in sales fail to follow up on opportunities. They provide a quotation for a product, send it to the customer and never find out what the customer thinks of it.

You have nothing to lose from following up. At the very least you may find out why the customer did not place an order and that might be helpful information. They may just have forgotten and your follow up prompts them to place the order. They may have a question about the order but were not sure how to get an answer. If you never follow up, you will reduce your chances of being successful.

**Standard Criteria**

To identify and manage opportunities consistently over time, we have to have a standard set of criteria against which we can judge them. These should be relevant to everyone and all opportunities so that they can be consistently applied and therefore all opportunities can be fairly ranked.

These criteria will vary from company to company and perhaps from product to product. If you sell a single product and there is only one group within each customer that might buy your product, then your definition of a good customer will go a long way to describing your good opportunities. However, once you have high graded all of your customers with opportunities, you probably require some more granularity in highlighting the best opportunities.

These criteria could include:
- How much revenue will we make?
- Are all the different buyers known?
- Is the budget known and understood?
- Have we worked with this customer previously?
- Are we the vendor that most matches their needs?
- How strong is the competition?
- How does our product fit with their existing infrastructure?

Possibly the most important of these is budget; is it known and understood? Too many sales opportunities are lost because the customer does not have the budget to buy the product. This is a question that needs to be asked early in the sales process to quickly qualify the opportunity. For products that are critical to a customer but for which they do not have defined budget, it can be amazing how quickly they can find the money if they try! Do not be put off by no budget but you must start to work with the customer to ensure that they can find it in time to do the deal.

Once we have identified all of the different criteria, we have to have a way of managing all of them so that more important criteria are given a greater weight. To that end, we have to determine which factors determine how valuable each opportunity is and then how important each of these factors is. To do this, we use the following process.

For each criterion, you have to define what a good opportunity looks like and what a poor opportunity looks like. Each of these then must have a number of points associated with it. By varying the maximum score, you can rank each of the criteria such that those that are more important give a bigger maximum score than those that are less important.

For example, you might decide that opportunities worth less than £10,000 are not worth chasing at all and that your best opportunities will be worth over £1m. In this instance, opportunities of less than £10,000 score 1 point and opportunities of more than £1m score 10 points with all others falling somewhere in between.

We then build a table such as Table 3, that defines all of our different criteria and their points range.

For each opportunity, you should then complete the reminder of the table and then calculate the total score for each one and then rank them. The comment column is there to add some context to your score, to explain why you gave it that score. Where actions can be identified to improve the opportunity, they should be scheduled to improve the chances of success.

*Value*

| Criteria | Poor | | Good | | Comment | Score | Action |
|---|---|---|---|---|---|---|---|
| Revenue | Less than £10,000 | 1 | More than £1m | 10 | | | |
| Different buyers known | Only met one person | 1 | Met and interviewed all relevant people | 10 | | | |
| Budget | Never asked about it | 1 | Known and available | 10 | | | |
| Worked with the customer previously | No | 1 | Yes | 4 | | | |
| Meeting most requirements | Less than 20% | 1 | More than 90% | 6 | | | |
| Competition | Very strong | 1 | We are the only supplier | 8 | | | |
| Fit with infrastructure | Poor, some customisation required | 1 | Fits right in | 5 | | | |

Table 3: Ranking Opportunities

139

Finally, once you have ranked all of your opportunities, you can start to focus on the most important ones. Of course, as you pursue opportunities, working through the identified actions, their ranking will change and their order of importance will similarly change. This means that you need to be regularly reviewing your list of opportunities and adjusting your activity accordingly. It will be important to pause or stop the pursuit of some and accelerate others over time. Do not continue to blindly pursue opportunities just because they were good six months ago!

**Forecasting**

Every sales person needs to forecast their predicted revenue. Revenue is the life blood of any company and drives decisions such as new investment, recruitment and expansion. As a result, an accurate and predictable revenue stream is important to every company. However, selling point products at irregular intervals leads to an uneven revenue stream. Consequently, a revenue forecast that accurately predicts the volume and timing of any deal is very important.

When starting in sales, it can be very difficult to make accurate forecasts. Sales people have a tendency to be too optimistic and therefore over forecast (and under deliver!). They do not have the experience to be confident when an opportunity will close. By focussing on the most promising opportunities and identifying the actions that are required to progress them, you will have the basis of a methodology that provides the greatest chance of success.

To be confident that you will be successful, you should take note of the requirements to reach a satisfactory closure, as detailed in Chapter 21, Closing.

# 18

## DIFFERENT BUYERS

*"The budget tells us what we can't afford, but it doesn't stop us from buying it"*
William Feather

E ach company will have different processes for making decisions and finalising purchases.

- Some make decisions by committee;
- Some managers decide for themselves;
- Some involve Procurement at the start, some at the end;
- Levels of budget authority vary.

It is very important that as you progress through the sales process, that you find out more and more of the information that you require regarding the decision-making process. It is very difficult to close a deal if you do not know who is going to sign the cheque at the end. If you do not find this information, you are likely to lose the sale. In this chapter, we look at how we deal with all of the different people involved in the purchasing process.

> You cannot close a deal if you do not know who is going to sign on behalf of the customer.

In almost every significant purchase that we make, different people are involved in the decision-making process. If we are buying a house, it may be a collective family decision. If you are buying on your own, you are likely to ask the opinion of family and friends before you buy. Even for a small purchase like a pair of jeans, you may ask a friend "does my bum look big in these?"

In the business to business world, there will almost certainly be multiple people and multiple roles involved in the decision-making process. Decision making is becoming increasingly complex and has to take account of multiple influences. Studies have shown that in a medium sized business (about 500 people), six to seven people are involved in any significant purchasing decision.

If you are trying to sell into such a company, it is important that you know not only how they will make a decision but who will be involved, what their role will be and what their opinion will be. Each person and role will have a different view on the purchase; they may each see different benefits that will come from the purchase. Any one of the decision makers could cause the deal to fail.

While you may not be able to meet everyone who is involved in a purchasing decision, getting to meet as many as possible will definitely help. You will have to understand their motivation, their role, their personality, their background and their position on the technology adoption curve. By understanding these things, you can give them the information that they require to make a decision, in a way that suits them and such that they understand the benefits of the purchase.

**Different Roles**

Each of the people involved in the purchase will have a different role to play. It is important in every sale to know which role each person is playing as the way we interact with them will vary. There are three primary roles:

1. Economic buyer
2. Technical buyer
3. End User

The Economic Buyer is the person who signs the cheque! They control the budget. Depending on the size of the purchase and the size of the company, their position will vary. For small companies, the CEO or CFO may have to approve all purchases. For larger companies, budget responsibility may be devolved down through the organisation.

Almost always, there is only ever one Economic Buyer. Most purchases come from a single budget or cost centre and that will only ever be controlled by one person. Only if a purchase is being paid for out of more than one budget will there be two economic buyers.

The Economic Buyer is usually the most difficult person to get to see as they are the most senior of all of the roles in the process. Quite often, other people in the process will prevent the sales person from meeting the economic buyer to maintain their own influence, over both the sale and the economic buyer. This is because the economic buyer will frequently not have in depth knowledge about every aspect of the business that they control. A department may employ multiple different skills and the manager is likely to have one of those skills but not all.

As a result, economic buyers will not be so interested in the different features and functions of your technology. However, they will very definitely care about value that it will bring. They will not want to sit through long presentations about how the technology works. They will want a short summary of how it is going to make their life better.

> Economic buyers will care most about the value your technology will deliver and care least about its features and functions.

The Technical Buyer is usually the most senior technical person reviewing the proposed product. They have the role because of their technical expertise. They will not have the ability to approve a deal but they can certainly say no to it! There is always one Technical Buyer, and possibly two, for any purchase.

Technical Buyers care that your product does what you claim it does. This is not about which button you press to start it but does it complete the processes that you have claimed in a reasonable and efficient way. They will want to know how it will fit in with other technologies, how long it will take to implement and how much training their team will require before they are effective users.

Technical buyers will often act like Economic Buyers and will often act as a gatekeeper to the Economic Buyer. This may frequently prevent you from getting to see the economic buyer. If the technical buyer is supportive, they may have to sell the product to the economic buyer on your behalf. To be successful, you will have to coach them to do this. The more support and information that you can give them to support the deal, the better; remembering at all times the economic buyer will want to know benefits not features.

The End User is the person most concerned with the user experience and day-to-day impact of your product. They do not have any budget and have the least influence on a decision. However, as they are the ones who will use the product, the success of the deal will depend on their success using the product.

There will be many End Users. They will vary in influence and will vary in how much they like your product. You do not require everyone to like it but you do require enough of them to like it. It will be unusual for a company to impose a product that the user community does not want.

End Users will be involved in product evaluations and trials. They will visit conferences and exhibitions to find new products to use. They will talk to friends and peers to find out more about particular products. They are more likely to be innovators, wanting new technology to work with but without ever thinking of the consequences of implementing it. Their enthusiasm for a new product can be misleading. Their desire to use new things can make a sales person think that they have a great opportunity for a deal when in reality it is far from such an opportunity.

It can be difficult for one person to meet with and relate to all of the different people involved in the deal. Frequently, the sales person will have their best relationship with the technical buyer. These are good starting points for determining if your product will be of benefit to an organisation. It may be difficult then to have as good a relationship with the users and the economic buyer. It may be appropriate to pair members of the sales team with the different buyers. So, technical consultants may spend time with the users and understand their needs and desires. At the appropriate time, it may be worthwhile introducing a sales manager or similar to the economic buyer.

However you choose to do it, you have to ensure that each of the people involved in the process are met and that their needs are understood. Any proposal must meet the needs of everyone involved.

**Customer Objectives**

The reason that you have reached this point of the sales process is that your customer has a need for your product. However, that customer is

> Each person involved in making the decision will have objectives to achieve, both professional and personal.

made up of individual people and each of them will be impacted in different ways by adopting your technology. Each person involved in the buying process will have objectives that they want to achieve as a result of the purchase. Moreover, they have business objectives – what does it mean for the business if we are successful? – and personal objectives – what does this mean for me personally if we are successful? Both objectives are important and will influence each decision maker. As a result, it is important to be aware of as many of them as possible so that you can address them in your proposal.

Business objectives should be fairly well aligned between the members of the team. They should all want the business to be successful, to deliver on its objectives and to be more productive. The understanding of these objectives will come more from the economic buyer than from the end users. They are typically measured by how successful they are in saving money and improving productivity. These are obviously the most important objectives to help to meet as ultimately, they drive the buying decision. You should have spent the majority of your time up to now finding and understanding each of these objectives. However, each person will also have personal objectives that will influence the way that they think. These are also important to try to understand and accommodate as much as you can.

Each person's formal goals will often be defined in their annual appraisal. However, they are equally likely to have informal goals such as a promotion, a bonus, an opportunity to work elsewhere or simply better recognition within the company. People are keen to be, and to be seen to be, successful. You only have to look at politicians to see how their political decisions are driven by their desire for personal success and promotion. Within companies, and particularly larger companies, there is the same political manoeuvring for success. This will have an impact on how each person makes decisions.

> The more that you can help individuals to achieve their goals, the more successful you are likely to be.

The more that you can help individuals to achieve their individual goals, the more successful you are likely to be. This applies to both their formal goals and their informal goals. As you get to know each person better, you will be able to ask them about their goals and how they are trying to achieve them. If your product can help them to achieve their goals, then it puts you in a much stronger position. If you find someone whose personal goals align with the successful implementation of your product, then they are a great ally to have as they will be as determined as you are to get the product installed and working.

You should not be afraid to ask about personal objectives. However, it would not be one of my first questions to a customer. This was discussed in Chapter 12, Asking Questions. You must build a strong bond with them first. The more that you have built trust with them, the more that they will open up to you and tell you information that is more personal than business. You also do not have to ask in a formal way. This is something that you can discuss over a coffee before or after a meeting. You might also invite your best contact out to lunch or similar. Out of the work setting, they are more likely to talk about their personal goals and tell you how you can help them to achieve them.

However you do this, the more information that you have, the better. This will inform your proposal and any subsequent negotiating strategy. If this is a complex sale with many parts, the negotiation will inevitably be important to success. Being aware of the different goals of all of the influencers on the final decision will greatly increase your chance of success.

**Different Behaviours**

Each of the roles in the buying process is occupied by a person and each person has a different personality. This personality will have an impact on how they behave during the process. It is very important to try to recognise their behaviour and adapt your behaviour to get the best out of the relationship.

There are all sorts of ways of classifying people's personalities and there are many books etc written about how to identify and work with all of them. I do not propose to go into a long analysis of all personality types here nor how they behave in all aspects of work. We will focus on how each behaviour type makes decisions as that is what we are asking them to do.

I strongly recommend building your understanding of personalities and behaviours. Sales are based on relationships and understanding the way that a person behaves will help you to have a better relationship with them. If you understand both your behaviour and their behaviour, you can modify your own to make them more comfortable in the relationship.

> Understanding how and why a person behaves the way that they do will lead to a better relationship all round.

The discussion that follows is all based on the analysis provided by TRACOM®. TRACOM® provides research-based learning solutions that improve an individual's ability to Think, Act and React. They refer to this as Social Intelligence. Social Intelligence combines positive psychology and neuroscience to help us overcome personal biases that affect our behaviour. Our performance improves as we learn to become more Versatile, Agile, Resilient and Emotionally Intelligent. More information can be found here, https://tracom.com/.

Our personality is a set of characteristics that uniquely influence our thoughts, motivations and behaviours. Our personality comes from both our genetics and our personal experience. It combines our ideas, values, hopes, dreams, attitudes, abilities plus our behaviour. Our behaviour is what we say and do and is only one component of our personality. However, it is what everyone else sees so is the most noticeable element of our personality. It is a bit like a pie, our personality is the filling and our behaviour is the pastry.

Our SOCIAL STYLE® is a pattern of actions that others can observe and agree upon for describing our behaviour. For example, are we quiet or loud; do we talk quickly or slowly; are we animated or controlled; do we lean forwards or backwards? These behaviours are habits we develop over our lifetime when interacting with one another. Once you know how a person prefers to behave, you can predict how that individual will probably behave in the future. Being able to anticipate the behaviour pattern enables you to build relationships by playing to strengths of that pattern and avoiding the weaknesses. There are four distinct SOCIAL STYLES, Driving, Expressive, Amiable and Analytical.

**Driving**. Driving style people are active, forceful and sometimes aggressive. They are focussed on goals and objectives that have to get done.

**Expressive**. Expressive style people are direct and seek to be involved in activities with others. They are active, spontaneous and make their presence known.

**Amiable**. Amiable style people are approachable, concerned and supportive. They are trusting in their personal relationships and unlikely to impose their views on others.

**Analytical**. Analytical style people are reserved, unaggressive and avoid appearing dominant. They can appear tentative and may not communicate unless they actually have to.

In terms of decision making, each SOCIAL STYLE has a different approach to making decisions.

Driving Style
- Willing to take risks and make quick decisions
- Formal, self-sufficient and usually deal with the reasoning and logic behind actions and decisions
- Need to be provided with facts, useful information and viable options;
- They like having power and making their own decisions

Expressive Style
- Quick to decide and make decisions based on intuition
- Focussed on the future, with intuitive visions and outspoken spontaneity
- May make mistakes and have frequent changes in direction and focus because of their desire to act on opinions, hunches and intuitions rather than facts and data
- Tends to take risks based on opinions so can be swayed by prominent people's support

Amiable Style
- Slow to decide and make decisions based on impacts on relationships

- Likely to stick with the comfortable and the known
- Likely to avoid decisions that might involve personal risks and conflict in relationships
- Value the input of others and will seek lots of feedback before making a decision

Analytical Style

- Slow to make decisions and act thoughtfully
- Likely to make decisions based on reason and logic
- Likely to live life according to facts, principles, processes, logic and consistency
- Makes decisions based on facts and data, never on opinions

If this analysis is of interest, I recommend working with TRACOM® to understand it further and see how it can help you to improve your interactions with other people. You should try to categorise each of the people involved based on their behaviours so that you can make appropriate proposals and react accordingly.

"SOCIAL STYLE® and the SOCIAL STYLE Model™ are the property of The TRACOM Group and are used with permission. Visit *www.tracom.com* to learn more."

**Cultural Differences**

In Chapter 5, Building Trust, we discussed cultural differences. For anyone who works across different countries, this is again important when we are dealing with the different people involved in the buying process. Different countries work in different ways and the people in those countries behave in a different way.

I will not repeat the content here. Suffice to say, different countries attitude to decision making will influence the way that companies go about making decisions. In a multi-national company, you may be dealing with many different nationalities for each purchase. Each of the dimensions of the national culture have an impact on decision making so ensure that you categorise each person based on their nationality. Many more details can be found here, *www.geerthofstede.com*

**Technology Adoption**

The technology adoption life cycle is a sociological model that describes the adoption or acceptance of a new product or innovation, according to the demographic and psychological characteristics of defined adopter groups. The process of adoption over time is typically illustrated as a classical normal distribution – as in the diagram below.

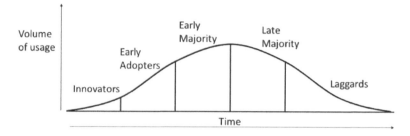

Figure 18.1: Technology Adoption Lifecycle

There is a longer description here:
*https://en.wikipedia.org/wiki/Technology_adoption_life_cycle*

The model indicates that the first group of people to use a new product is called "Innovators," followed by "Early Adopters". Next come the "Early Majority" and "Late Majority". The last group to eventually adopt a product are called "Laggards". We can make some general descriptions of each of these groups.

Innovators (2.5%) tend to be better educated, reasonably prosperous and more risk-oriented than other people. They will frequently buy new technology because it is new, regardless of whether they need it or if it is any good. They take the risk that it will work because they want to be first person to have it. These are the people who will queue overnight to buy the next version of the iPhone.

Early Adopters (13.5%) are younger and better educated people. They are not necessarily wealthy but want use new technology as soon as they can afford it. They will have to buy a product in order for it to be successful. They will probably buy the latest version of the iPhone when they renew their contract.

Early Majority (34%) are more conservative but open to new ideas. They will like new technology but will wait for it to be proven before they adopt it. They will use an iPhone but are not so concerned as to what version they use.

Late Majority (34%) are older, often less educated and fairly conservative in their views. They may have grown up without much technology so tend to be wary of using it. They will probably only have a standard mobile phone, not a smart phone.

Laggards (16%) are very conservative and are the oldest group. They probably do not even have a mobile phone or if they do, it will not be a smart phone.

In his book "Crossing the Chasm", Geoffrey Moore proposes a variation to the original lifecycle. He suggests that for new technology, there is a gap or chasm somewhere in the middle of the Early Adopters. Getting a new product adopted requires it to "cross the chasm" by getting all of the Early Adopters to use it. The Early Adopters are therefore critical to the success of any product. No product can be successful without them as sufficient payback only really comes once the Early Majority start to adopt it.

Early Adopters can be extremely important in other ways. They will generally provide considerable and candid feedback on the product which can influence its development. Versions 2 and 3 of any product are frequently significant upgrades on version 1 and it is often only when these versions are released that the Early Majority take notice of it. These developments come from the feedback from the Early Adopters. This feedback is not without a cost, however, as the Early Adopters will often want significant support and assistance in the early stages.

> Having the support of Early Adopters is often crucial to getting new technology adopted in a company.

Interestingly, Innovators are less important to the success of a product. Firstly, there are fewer of them. However, more importantly, once they have bought it, they are equally quick to discard it and move on to the next innovation. Their motivation for buying is newness rather than functionality.

In any sales opportunity, it is important to understand both what personalities you are dealing with and where your product is in the technology adoption lifecycle. If you have only just launched it, you must look for innovators and early adopters. It is fairly pointless talking to laggards at this stage as they will just not be interested. Conversely, if your product has been around for a number of years and is widely used, it is Late Majority and Laggards that you have to identify.

This classification by technology adoption can also apply to whole companies. A company may have a reputation as an innovative, early adopter or it may be very conservative and only adopt technology once every other company is using it. This is an important characteristic that you should be aware of. I am cautious of believing all companies whose strategy states that they will adopt the latest technology. My experience is that this is not often the case. You should judge a company by its actions rather than by words on a webpage.

If you are launching a new product, it is important to get quality feedback as early as possible to refine its development. To achieve this, it is often necessary to work directly with an Early Adopter. This can be beneficial to both parties. The vendor gets quality feedback; the customer gets early access to the technology with the advantages that it brings.

There is obviously a risk for the Early Adopter as the product may not be fully functional or work without support. They therefore require a large amount of support in the early stages of deployment and use. In addition, they may be given very preferential pricing to make the disruption worthwhile. In return, the vendor will get experience in deployment and usage plus significant promotional material from a known customer. This can be of significant value.

**Characterising your Customer**

Once you are progressing with an opportunity and are getting to know the people involved, you should try to document each of these people, the role that they play and their personality, as much as you can. Firstly, this will help you to identify if you have met with all of the people involved. Secondly, you can plan your strategy to close the deal based on their objectives and personality. Try to build a table such as the following to document your findings.

| Name | What is the name of the person |
|---|---|
| Role | What is their role in the company? |
| Pair | Who is the best person within the selling team to meet with them on a regular basis? |
| Buyer Type | Are they the economic buyer, technical buyer or end user? |
| Business Objectives | What business objectives are they trying to solve? |
| Personal Objectives | What are their personal objectives and how does that influence their thinking? |
| SOCIAL STYLE | What is their SOCIAL STYLE and how does this influence how they make decisions? |
| Culture | Where are they from and does that impact the way that they make decisions? |
| Adopter | Where do they fit on the technology adoption lifecycle and how does that fit with your product? |

Table 4: Characterising your customer

Once you have done this for everyone in the buying process, you will be in a great position to tailor your message to each of the people involved to ensure that you help them to meet their objectives and make it easy for them to make a decision.

# 19

## PROPOSALS

*"I lay it down as a general rule, Harriet, that if a woman doubts as to whether she should accept a man or not, she certainly ought to refuse him. If she can hesitate as to '"Yes,'" she ought to say '"No'" directly. It is not a state to be safely entered into with doubtful feelings, with half a heart."*
Jane Austen, Emma

Your proposal is where everything that you have done in the sales process comes together and you commit to paper the offer that you are making to your customer. It must demonstrate that you understand the customer and that you can help them. Most importantly, it has to demonstrate that their business will be better off by having your product and that you can prove this.

We discussed proposals somewhat in Chapter 10, Presentations. A sales presentation is essentially just a presentation of your proposal. If you can get the opportunity to present your proposal, take it! Your customer is buying you as much as they are buying your product. When you present your proposal, you provide a human face to the product. With a presentation, you get immediate feedback, the opportunity to answer questions and, if required, to revise aspects of the proposal. You also have a wider audience which is hopefully paying attention to all aspects of your presentation. Many people have a tendency to skim read proposals and may miss critical pieces of information. If you present the proposal, then this is less likely to happen and everyone will have the same level of understanding. However, this is not always possible and you have to provide a document that defines your offer.

If you are selling a physical item, such are hardware, or computer software, then your proposal might simply be a quotation. However, for anything that involves different elements, and certainly if it contains services, then a more complicated document is required.

**Focus on the customer**

Imagine being at a party where you end up with someone and all they do is talk about themselves. It is boring isn't it? Most people will try to make their excuses and leave. If your proposal is just about your company and your product then you are doing exactly the same thing. Your customer will not be engaged by the proposal and will fail to appreciate it.

Throughout the sales process, you have spent a lot of time researching your customer's activity and finding out about their needs. You have to demonstrate that you understand these things. The perfect proposal effectively states:

"I understand what you want to achieve and what you need as a result. This is how I can help you to achieve your objectives and overcome your problems in the simplest and most cost-effective way."

When your customer reads your proposal, it should reflect everything that they have told you. If you only ever talk about your company and your product, how interesting is that for the customer?

> Your proposal should be focussed on your customer and how you are going to help them, not on your technology.

Remember that they are not buying your product, they are buying the value that it brings to them. You have to focus on how they are going to get that value, not the features and functions of your product.

To achieve this, you should write a new proposal for every new opportunity. Every customer and every sale is different and your proposal should address the specifics of the particular needs that the customer has. It should not include standard text or marketing brochures. These are deliberately general. The proposal should not include list prices or price schedules. Again, they are not specific to your customer. Everything you write should make the customer feel that they are the most important customer in the world.

Your proposal should be the final thing to make the customer say "yes". It should respond to all of their needs and have an answer for all of them. It must be compelling, engaging and enlightening

The proposal must be able to stand on its own. It is highly likely that it will be given to someone who you have not met or had the chance to question. As a result, it has to be fully understandable for someone who has not been engaged in the process. They should have only a minimal number of questions at the end of reading it.

A very useful book about proposals is "Powerful Proposals" by David Pugh and Terry Bacon, see References.

**Proposal Contents**

A business proposal contains five essential elements.
1. The objectives – what is the company trying to achieve?
2. The needs – what is stopping the company from achieving the objectives?
3. The features – what product will you provide that helps them?
4. The benefits – how will the company be better off as a result?
5. The proof – how can you prove that this will happen?

This is exactly the same structure as a story.
1. The objectives = the setting of the story
2. The needs = the complication
3. The features = the turning point
4. The benefits = the resolution.

We remember stories much more than we remember facts. We understand stories better; remember them more accurately, and we find them more engaging to read. So, by ordering the proposal in the same way, we engage with the reader much more and have a greater chance of being successful.

**Objectives.** This section covers the objectives of the company, what they are trying to achieve? While you obviously have to focus on the objectives that you can help them to accomplish, bear in mind that they have many more objectives. These may be as important or more important to the reader and will therefore have an impact on their decision.

**Needs**. This section details the reasons why the company is struggling to meet its objectives. Again, be mindful that there are more than you can help with.

**Features**. This is the only time you get to write about your product. There is a temptation to provide a large amount of detail but this should be resisted. Provide as much detail as you require in the body of the document with backup information in appendices. Remember that not everyone who reads the document will be fully conversant with the technology. You need to have enough detail to demonstrate what it does but not too much that it swamps the most important section, benefits.

**Benefits**. This is the critical part of the proposal. This is ultimately what the customer is buying. Ensure that you stress the areas and impacts that you excel at but your competitors do not. This is how you differentiate yourself from the competition.

**Proof**. This is the "non-story" part of the proposal and is very factual. It is included to demonstrate that you can do what you claim to be able to do.

Clearly, these are not the only things that have to go into a proposal. However, they must be in all proposals. The rest of the contents will vary depending on your product and what you are actually proposing.

**Proposal Structure**

I do not recommend using each of these headings as sections in a proposal. They are too blunt to be used like that. Quite how you structure a proposal will depend on your company philosophy and formats as well as the product that you are selling. I tend to have the following sections as a minimum:

1. Introduction – This sets the scene; it could be simply just a description of the customer and your company; it could contain some of the objectives at a very high level.

2. Current Situation – this describes the current position of the customer and includes both the objectives and needs.

3. Proposal – this describes what you will do for the customer. This is where you write about the features you are providing. In a basic proposal, it may also contain the proof.

4.  Costs – this defines what you will charge the customer

5.  Benefits – this defines the benefits that they will receive from buying the product

6.  Terms and conditions – there are any commercial or legal terms that have to be included. If there are long, legal terms to be included, these should be in an appendix. Any critical or unusual terms and conditions should be highlighted in the main proposal.

7.  Agreement – an area to allow the customer to sign to accept the proposal

Some additional sections that might be useful to include are:

1.  Timing – when will you deliver the product

2.  Staffing – who will be involved in delivering services

3.  Scope – if services are included, what is in scope and what is out of scope is important to be included to ensure that both the customer and yourselves are in agreement.

4.  Data Available – if the services include some form of interpretation, then the data that is available is important to define, again to set expectations

5.  Deliverables – This could be part of the proposal but it may be necessary to explicitly define what the customer will receive so that all parties are in agreement. It may be necessary to define some quality criteria for each deliverable if there is a potential range of these.

6.  Constraints, Assumptions and Dependencies – in complicated projects, these may be necessary to define to ensure that both parties understand the basis under which the proposal was constructed. It is sometimes necessary to be explicit about parameters under which any project is under taken.

7.  Expiry date – always include an expiry date, even if it seems irrelevant. It may be important if there are time sensitive prices included or limited availability of personnel for a project.

This by no means covers all aspects of writing a proposal. This chapter is included to try to tie the elements of this book into the proposal. The format, structure and content of any proposal will be dictated by products that it relates to and each individual company.

# 20

# NEGOTIATION

*"Everything is negotiable. Whether or not the negotiation is easy is another thing."*
Carrie Fisher

If you have reached this stage of the sales process, well done! You have done your job. While the deal may not be closed, your customer almost certainly wants what you have to sell. Why would they bother to negotiate with you if they do not want it? Negotiation takes time and money. No one has enough of both of these to waste just to irritate a supplier. So, congratulations, you have a deal! Quite what the final arrangements will be are yet to be decided and the deal could fall through but you have to try really hard to lose a deal from here. Provided you have set expectations correctly and understand what is important to your customer, you should come away with a deal.

> If your customer is negotiating with you, it is highly likely that they want to buy your solution.

The role of the sales person also changes slightly during a negotiation. The sales person is often the middle person, representing their company to the customer and representing the customer to their company. The sales person is really the only person who fully understands both sides. Their sales manager wants a deal with the highest price, their customer wants a deal with the lowest price. The sales person has to balance both requirements to get the best deal for both sides and this can be a strange position when they first encounter it. Again, a positive solution for both sides will be reached through an understanding of the needs of both sides. We have discussed at length how to understand the needs of the customer, so ensure that you find the time to understand the needs of your manager!

If you search Amazon Books for Negotiation, there are over 10,000 items listed. I do not intend to try to improve on any of those in this book. This book is about sales, of which negotiation is just a part.

Compared to inter government treaties, sales negotiations are extremely easy as both sides want the same thing – they both want the sale to complete. However, that does not mean that the negotiations are not difficult at times. So, we will look at negotiations from the perspective of the sales person and how they should approach them.

Negotiation is the process of movement to reach an agreement that is fair to both sides. Negotiation must result in a win-win agreement. This does not mean that both sides get everything that they want – that would be almost impossible. However, both sides have to be happy with the result.

Negotiation does not involve one side being dominant such that the other side does not achieve their objectives. One side cannot insist on being right. Give and take is required. If both sides are too far apart to reach an agreement, then deadlock may be the result. This is not in the interest of either side. However, as long as expectations have been correctly set, this should not happen.

Negotiation is definitely not about one side getting everything that they want and the other getting nothing. This is definitely not a win-win agreement. This results in either an unhappy customer who never buys from the seller again or an unhappy sales team who have no interest in helping the customer to be successful. You want your customer to be your customer for ever, not just for this sale.

> Negotiation is a process; it requires give and take for both sides to be happy at the end.

Negotiations may start to involve other people within a company. Many customers will have a procurement department that is responsible for buying products. Indeed, I know some companies where the Economic Buyer is not allowed to discuss the price of a product; this must be done by procurement. This is to avoid the possibility of bribery and corruption so is a reasonable practice for the customer. However, it introduces significant complications for the sales person and often for the Economic Buyer.

Procurement's role is to acquire the product at the lowest cost and with the least commitment on their behalf. They are not the end user of the product so frequently do not understand the value of it. So, when you have spent all of your time selling value, all of a sudden you are dealing with a group who are just focussed on price. It is very difficult to avoid this scenario if it is the practice within your customer; all you can do is to minimise the impact.

To do this, you have to be absolutely sure that you understand everything that is driving the customer to buy your product and what value they will derive from it. If negotiations get difficult, you can keep focussed on the value and use the knowledge that you have about the customer to dictate terms. In the end, procurement will be forced to consult with the economic buyer who will hopefully understand the value and reasons for your offer.

I was once negotiating with procurement of a company for a deal to close just before the end of the year. Procurement felt that it would be better to wait till the new year to complete the deal or get a better deal. However, I knew that the economic buyer had budget to make the purchase this year but would not have it the following year. As a result, I was able to hold my ground and not offer any further concessions as I knew that they needed to complete the deal quickly.

This is why it is so important to understand as much as you possibly can about the buyer and their needs in advance of making an offer. You can tailor the offer to those needs and constraints to leave them little room for negotiation.

**Objections**

Objections can occur at any stage in the sales process but come more at the start and end than at any stage in between. During the negotiations, a customer might object to any number of things that you propose. By this stage in the sales process, we have invested a lot of time and emotional energy in the deal and can almost smell the cheque! As such, we have a tendency for objections to be taken personally, as an attack on ourselves. They are anything but that.

Brian Tracy (*www.briantracy.com*) said "Treat objections as requests for further information." If your customer is objecting, then it probably means that they are thinking seriously about how your product will work within their organisation. They might not have done this prior to this stage. An objection is not "no!" You customer probably wants to move forwards, they just require further clarification or reassurance. The objection may be driven by a lack of understanding or possibly a need that you have not uncovered before now.

There are four steps to handling an objection:

1. Pause – allow the customer to finish objecting before you say anything and pause again!
2. Understand thoroughly – clarify what is driving them to make the objection;
3. Respond thoughtfully – make a considered response, even at a later time if required;
4. Confirm agreement – be completely confident that the customer has been reassured and that the objection has been dealt with.

**Pause.** There is a tendency to jump in and start to deal with the objection before your customer has finished speaking. This comes from taking it personally. Take your time. Pause. Take a deep breath and then answer. Thank the customer for raising the problem; it is important that all problems are dealt with before a deal is completed. Say something that shows that you care about the problem, even if you think that their objection is ridiculous! Demonstrating that you care about your customer's needs show you care about them as a person.

**Understand Thoroughly.** Before you can properly respond, you have to fully understand the issue. You will have to question your customer using the same techniques that we discussed in Chapter 12, Asking Questions. Ask open questions that get to the heart of the problem. Once you have isolated the problem, confirm that you have understood by repeating it back to the customer in your own words.

**Respond Thoughtfully.** Consider your response before you speak. This is something that matters to your customer so it should matter to you. Your response will be driven by the problem that the customer has raised so ensure that you respond to the problem rather than any side issue or specific language that your customer has used. If you are not sure of the best response, agree to put it to the side and that you will come back with an answer as soon as you can.

**Confirm Agreement.** Once you have finished speaking, give the customer a chance to respond. Before you move on to anything else, ensure that they are happy with the response and that their objection has been dealt with. If not, you may have to go back though the process of understanding and responding before you move on.

# 21

## CLOSING

*"When a man tells me he is going to put all his cards on the table, I always look up his sleeve."*
Lord Hore-Belisha

Closing is considered by some people to be the most difficult part of the sales process. Getting the customer to say "yes". I think that it is the easiest part. However, that statement comes with a small get out clause! It is only easy if you have done all other parts of the sales process well. Then, closing is easy. If you have not done everything else well, then indeed, closing will be difficult because the customer is not ready to say "yes".

> Closing is easy if you have done the rest of the process correctly.

If you have done your job well enough and followed the sales process, you have a deal and all you have to do is get a signature. Your negotiations are there to finalise details and handle objections; once they are finished, you should be able to shake hands on a deal. Closing is really just about getting the paperwork finalised.

If you ever watch the BBC (and other networks) television show, The Apprentice, you will see many of the candidates claim to be great closers. What they really mean is that they can negotiate a deal (in reality just haggling over the price) and then shake hands. They are not closing, they are negotiating.

Imagine you (as a single person) meet an attractive person in a bar and get talking. After an hour or so, you are getting on very well and they seem to like you. Would you ask them to marry you at that point? I doubt it. The next questions should be "can I have your contact details please?" or "can I see you again, please?" It is far too soon to try to close the deal! It is exactly the same in sales.

There is an old saying (immortalised in the movie Glengarry Glen Ross) that sales people should always be closing. That may have been fine when sales people went door to door and could not afford to waste time with someone who was not going to buy. Today, closing is as much about moving to the next stage of the sales process as it is about closing the deal.

We have discussed how at every stage in the sales process you have to be selling the next stage which means that you have to close the current stage. As your customer gets used to saying yes to the next stage, they get closer to saying yes to your product. They make small, intermediate steps to reach the end goal rather than one giant leap.

So, closing is about confirming the next step in the sales process as well as closing the deal at the end of the process. There are many different techniques for gaining agreement, no matter what stage of the process you are at. Not all are appropriate to business to business technology sales and certainly not to closing the next step in the process. We will review just a few of them that can prove useful.

**Closing Techniques**

**Assumptive close**. In this scenario, the sales person just assumes that the customer is happy to move to the next stage or to do the deal. They might say "I'll set up a meeting next week then;" or "who should I talk to in order to get that agreed?"

**Negative assumption close**. Here the sales person asks "is there any reason not to move to the next stage?" This has two effects. It draws out any objections that the customer may have and then, if the question is asked often enough, leaves the customer with nowhere to go other than to say "yes."

**Direct close.** As you might expect, in this scenario, the sales person just asks a direct question to get the customer to agree. "Would you like to buy?" for example. This is perfectly reasonable if you have a good relationship with the customer and you are confident that they are ready to make a decision. I advise against asking such a question if you are not certain of the answer.

**Indirect close.** Not quite the opposite of the direct close but in this scenario the sales person asks an indirect question to try to solicit a positive response. For example, "are you happy with this agreement?"

**Sharp angle close.** This can come towards the end of the negotiation process. If the customer asks for a commitment from the sales person, such as "can you deliver tomorrow?" The sales person can respond with a request to close the deal, saying "If I promise that, will you sign the deal?" This is good to ensure that all objections are overcome and leaves the customer will little room to move if you promise to deliver what is important to them.

**Possibility of loss close.** This is used regularly towards the end of a quarter or sales year. The sales person offers a special deal with a limited availability to pressure the customer into making a commitment. This can also work with products that have a limited shelf life or availability.

Customers are getting more and more familiar with closing techniques and have often received training in how to deal with sales people. As a result, many closing techniques do not work and are viewed with suspicion. Again, if you have done everything right up to this point, the customer should be desperate to buy from you and will be asking you for the deal rather than the other way around. Be careful about how and when you use the closing techniques. If in doubt, the direct close is the simplest method and if you have a good relationship with your customer, should work every time.

**Revenue Recognition**

For many years, I sold software on behalf of US companies. These companies had to comply with a specific set of requirements, known as the Generally Accepted Accounting Principles (GAAP) which meant that I had to comply with them. While they are not universal, they are a very useful way of ensuring that you have done everything you have to do to close a deal and most importantly, recognise the revenue and get paid.

The GAAP principles state that for revenue to be recognised, there must be:

1. Persuasive evidence of an arrangement.
2. Delivery must have occurred
3. The sales price must be fixed or determinable.
4. Collectability is reasonably assured.

Persuasive evidence of an arrangement is a document signed by both parties that defines what has been sold, by whom, to whom and for how much. This might just be a signed quotation for a single product or a purchase order issued by the customer. These documents will generally have terms and conditions associated with them that cover the financial and legal obligations of both sides.

The product must have been delivered to the customer. If the product is a software license, then emailing it to the customer is usually sufficient. However, if it is a consulting project, then the work must be done before the revenue is recognised. Just because you have been paid, it does not mean that you can recognise the revenue.

If you sell a single product for a fixed price, then the sales price is easily fixed. However, if you sell two products for a single price, the sales price of each is not determinable. This may not be a problem if both have been delivered. However, if one has been delivered and one has not, then the revenue for neither product can be recognised which may be a problem. For a long consulting project, if you have agreed a fixed fee, then nothing can be recognised till the whole project is complete as the fee for individual stages cannot be fixed. Try breaking these projects into stages to ensure that the revenue can be recognised as you proceed.

You are assured of collectability if you are confident that you will get paid. Most agreements give the customer time to pay so they have both the product and their money for a period. Not all customers pay on time so you have to be confident that they will pay eventually. Most sales organisations will perform some form of credit check before agreeing to sell to a new customer. Once a customer has paid once, a track record of payment is usually sufficient assurance. If you cannot get this assurance, then it may be appropriate to ask for payment in advance.

While these principles will not govern all companies and agreements and every sales organisation will have their own policies, they are a useful check list to ensure that you are going to complete a satisfactory deal for all parties. For complicated deals, it is important to engage with finance managers, legal department and compliance to ensure that deals are satisfactory based on the accounting principles that you have to comply with.

**Closing the Deal**

In simple terms, to close a deal, you have to get a signed agreement, deliver your product and get paid. In reality, you have to understand a variety of things to ensure that you are in a position to close the deal when you and your customer want to. You have to:

- Know what you are selling and for how much;
- Be certain that they have the budget to buy;
- Know why and when the customer needs the product;
- Understand the company's decision-making process;
- Know who is involved in the customer approval process;
- Have handled any objections;
- Be certain that you have understood the competition and how you relate to them;
- Involve legal, finance and compliance as required;
- Negotiate with procurement if required;
- Most importantly, know who signs the deal.

You may think that it is obvious what you are selling and for how much but quite often there can be confusion, particularly if it is a complicated solution or combination of products. You will naturally understand your products in great detail but your customer will not. The nuances of your offer may not be clear, particularly to people not involved in the process up this point. Try to ensure that it is as simply stated as possible. If it is a complex consulting project, there will have to be complete agreement on all aspects of the project before you can finalise the whole agreement.

How you price the deal will depend on many factors such as what products are involved and how they are individually priced. You may want to just provide a single price or a price per item. However you do this, you have to be certain that the customer has sufficient budget to pay. This is something that you should have found out early in the sales process so that you can correctly price your offer.

If you try to close a deal without knowing why and when your customer wants the product, you are setting yourself up for failure. This is the most important thing to establish at the start of the process and we discussed it at length in the chapters on Needs, Chapters 11-13.

No two companies make decisions in the same way. In some, a manager will make the decision and buy as they see fit. In others, a whole group of people will be involved in making the decision. How they make a decision will impact who you have to deal with in advance. It is often easier to only have to deal with one decision maker. However, that is then a binary decision, do they agree or not. With a committee, you will have to work harder but you do not have to persuade everyone on the merits of the deal.

Once you have understood their decision-making process, you have to identify each of the economic and technical buyers and follow the process from Chapter 18, Different Buyers. What is important to each of them and have you addressed it in your proposal?

Are you confident that there are no more objections? At this stage, you can reasonably ask "Is there anything else I should know?"; "Is there anything to stop this deal from happening?" or "Is there anything else you are not happy about?" If there are no more objections, your customer should be in a position to say yes to the deal.

In any large, complex deal, there are likely to be legal and financial implications for your company. It is worth involving legal, finance and compliance departments as early as is reasonable. Do not leave it till the day before the customer is due to sign! The agreement document should be all agreed internally before you present it to the customer for signature. You do not look like very professional if you present an agreement and then have to withdraw it because it is not compliant. In some deals, it is easier to connect the legal and financial departments of your company and that of your customer and allow them to negotiate directly on the relevant clauses in an agreement. Being in the middle just slows down the process.

The customer may appoint a single point of contact within their procurement department to conduct all of the negotiations. They will work with their legal and financial departments to respond to parts of your agreement. As we discussed in Chapter 20, Negotiation, procurement departments are usually measured in a different way to your main contacts. They are not interested in value, just price, so will approach the agreement in a very different way.

The last thing to do is to get the deal signed. There is usually only one person who is allowed to do this from the customer company. They are usually the budget holder who will be paying for the product. As we discussed in Chapter 18, Different Buyers, they can be difficult to get to meet. We have to rely on our contact to present the deal in a way that persuades the budget holder to accept. This can be difficult as they are not used to "selling".

It is worth spending time with your main contact, who will present the deal internally, to coach them to present the deal in a way that maximises the chances of success. Focus on the value over everything else. Talk about how other companies have implemented the product successfully. Ask if there are typical things that the economic buyer will want to understand so that you can address those.

If you have managed to do all of this successfully, then you should expect to get a signed agreement and your deal is done. Congratulations!

# Examples
# and
# Exercises

## INTRODUCTION

I have tried to keep the book as straight forward as possible. Since each company will have its own sales process and each product will have its own features and benefits, it is not possible to be too prescriptive. I have written about the basic activities that a sales person must do in order to be effective and efficient. You will have to take these and apply them to your company, your processes and your products.

These examples and exercises are designed to help you to do this. Sales is an activity and you have to practise it in order to get better. There are worked examples using a fictitious technology company and a series of activity sheets. These are there so that you can immediately apply the theory to your own products and customers.

You will require time and space to work on your skills and continue to apply the lessons from the book to your weekly and monthly activities. The examples will provide you with ideas to get you started; the exercises will help you to apply them to your product.

There are further sales activities that are not included in this section as they require other people to be involved. For these, you should seek the help of colleagues in order to practise. You should practise as much as possible in order to get better. Every professional sports person trains and practises. It should be no different for a professional sales person. Only with constant practise can you get better over time. I strongly urge you to take the time to work with others to improve your skills.

## TECHNOLOGY EXAMPLE

In trying to make this book as practical as possible, I wanted to provide a worked example so that you can see how a technology sales person might go about completing many of the actions that are discussed. The person and company are entirely fictitious although clearly such people and companies do exist. They are essentially a blend of many people and companies and are presented for illustrative purposes only.

### Meet Sam

Sam is a sales person for TRIC Software. Sam has a degree in psychology and 11 years of work experience. Sam initially started to work for a market research company, working on opinion polls and focus groups. After five years working there, Sam moved to TRIC Software working as an inside sales person, answering the phone to enquiries and following up leads across all software products. After two years in that role, Sam moved into a new sales role, actively pursuing new customers and finding new opportunities for their payroll software, PayDay.

### TRIC Software

TRIC Software is based in Leicester, UK and employs over 200 people. It provides a variety of software products around people management and HR functions. PayDay is their payroll software that manages the payment of employee wages. All companies will pay their employees a salary and so must "run payroll". This requires them to define a person's wages, calculate what tax they are due to pay, identify any other deductions or payments that they must make and generate a payslip stating what the employee has been paid and what has been deducted. PayDay was developed in response to customer needs to replace a largely manual / spreadsheet driven processes which took a long time and were prone to user error. Any changes to legislation and taxation required many changes to these processes and created a lot of work for HR each year. PayDay solves many of these problems for customers with a single programme to manage all of this process.

Some features of PayDay are:

- It runs in the cloud with full security complying with international standards

- It manages all aspects of an employee's pay in a single database

- It is automatically updated with tax and benefit rules from each country

- It integrates with major accounting software packages

- It can run on PC or tablet

- Payroll processing can be performed for any period or group of employees at any time

- It automatically emails payslips to employees

- It allows employees to login to update their personal information and holidays

- Software is GDPR compliant

- It is ISO 27001 and ISO 9001 compliant

- Links to banking software to drive employee payments

- Provides a management dashboard for analysis and audit.

The software is leased to the customer, they never own a perpetual license to use it. Customers pay for the software based on the total number of employees that they have at the start of each year. This provides them access to the complete software package. The price per employee varies by country depending on the complexity of the tax and benefit rules in each country.

## BUILDING A SALES PROCESS

To help you to build your sales process, I suggest that you think about your activities in each of these stages.

Stage 1 – Suspect – I think that there might be an opportunity.

Stage 2 – Prospect – I know that there is an opportunity

Stage 3 – Opportunity – I have made the customer a proposal

Stage 4 – Sale – I have closed the deal.

In Stage 1, we generate ideas of where there may be an opportunity; this requires us to research our customers and identify potential needs.

In Stage 2, we go and talk to the customer and confirm that there is a valid opportunity.

In Stage 3, we make a proposal / give a presentation of how we can satisfy the needs of the customer.

In Stage 4, we negotiate if required and close the deal.

Use the boxes on the next page to record your activities in each of them. You will probably find that there are a lot more activities per opportunity in Stages 1 and 2 than there are in 3 and 4. This is because there are many more things that we need to do to generate opportunities than we need to do to close them. You will find that you will add to this list on a regular basis as you work through the book.

**Exercise – Building a Sales Process**

| Suspect | Prospect |
|---|---|
| | |
| Opportunity | Sale |
| | |

## BUILDING TRUST

In business, we have to trust the people that we do business with. Without that, we are unlikely to be successful. So, the first job for any sales person is to build that trust, it does not come automatically.

### Strategies for Building Trust

There are a number of simple strategies for building trust.

- Say what you are going to do and then do what you say!
- Communicate, communicate, communicate.
- Appreciate long term relationships more than short term success.
- Be honest!
- Always do the right thing.
- Coach your customers.

These are mostly reactive strategies. To be successful, you should look to proactively work with your customers to build a high level of trust. Some actions that you can take that can help to do that are:

- Send them useful information / technical papers;
- Invite them for coffee / lunch without any sales agenda;
- Have user group meetings where they can talk to experts and other users;
- Provide regular tips and hints on the use of the technology.

Think about the things that you can do to help to build trust with your customers. There is an example of what Sam does. Use the worksheet to record your proposed activities.

You may find that some activities are more successful than others. It is worth reviewing your activities on a regular basis to decide which to do more of and which to possible do less of.

**Example**

These are ten things that Sam regularly does to build trust with customers.

1. Sam has learnt how to use the software in great detail so if a customer talks about features and functions during a meeting, Sam is often able to help them. Sam knows that good product knowledge helps to build trust.

2. Sam meets all existing customers twice per year to review their use of the software and to inform them of upcoming developments. Sam uses these meetings to understand changes in employee numbers as this drives the revenue forecast to management.

3. Sam arranges for a tax and benefit specialist to visit each customer once per year to explain changes in legislation and their impact on employees. This is provided for free.

4. All of Sam's customers are invited to an annual user group meeting where they get to mix with other customers and attend a gala dinner.

5. The company regularly issues a review of best practise which Sam sends to all customers.

6. Sam sends a *Hints and Tips* email to all software users each month.

7. After each customer meeting, Sam documents what was discussed and notes any actions. Sam immediately sends a *Thank You* email to the customer noting any specific actions. Sam tries to ensure that all actions are completed within two weeks and notified to the customer.

8. Sam follows all customers on LinkedIn and likes and comments on their posts.

9. Whenever Sam's customer makes a public announcement, Sam contacts them with an appropriate comment, "Congratulations...." Or "I'm sorry to hear....".

10. Before meeting a new customer, Sam researches the person as much as possible and talks about something relevant soon after they meet.

**Exercise - Tactics for Building Trust**

What are ten things that you can do to help to build trust with your customer?

1

2

3

4

5

6

7

8

9

10

## WHY DO YOU DO WHAT YOU DO?

To help to build trust and inspire confidence in you as a sales person, you need to be able to explain why you are in your current role. People follow great leaders because of why they are doing something not because of what they are doing. This is important for anyone in any job but is even more important in sales.

Why you do something is not for the end result. Businesses make a profit but that is not why they exist. They exist because a small number of people thought that they could make a difference. They were inspired to do something different. There is a reason why you decided to sell this product over any other.

You need to create a story based on:

- When did you start this role?
- What were you doing before this role?
- What was the trigger for ending that?
- What made you want to do this current role?
- What inspires you?
- What is it about the product that you sell that that excites you?
- Why are you different?

You will probably have a number of different versions of this story and will choose the most appropriate for each situation that you are in. Start by reviewing Sam's responses and story, then do it for yourself. Try to repeat this a few times so that you can create a number of different versions of it.

The story should take 1-2 minutes to tell, no more. The story should contain the following:

A sequence. The events that you recount should happen one after another.

A framework. This should contain the following:

A Setting – a time and a place, so that we can locate it.

A Complication – something unexpected happens

A Turning point – the hero finds a solution

A Resolution – everyone lives happily ever after.

The story must be interesting and unpredictable to keep us interested and guessing what will happen next.

The story should revolve around a main character. In your story, this is you!


## Example – Sam's story

When did you start this role?

*I started 3 years ago.*

What were you doing before this role?

*I was working inside sales, following up leads from people who had contacted us via our website.*

What was the trigger for ending that?

*This was a new role and offered to the whole team to apply for. Four of us applied and I was selected.*

What made you want to do this current role?

*I was keen to be more proactive; I didn't like being tied to the same desk every day; I wanted to use the sales skills that I had learnt.*

What inspires you?

*I really like helping people. Customers come to us because they have a problem and we are able to improve their workflows.*

What is it about the product that you sell that that excites you?

*The first company that I worked for was always getting our pay incorrect. We got paid overtime and overnight allowances so our pay was always different every month. They used a spreadsheet to calculate salary and always got it wrong. We were for ever having to check it. PayDay makes everything so much simpler for HR to enter the right data and for employees to get paid correctly. It makes everyone happy and that makes me happy.*

Why are you different?

*My degree in psychology taught me about how and why people react to different situations. I get to apply this learning to what I do in sales much more than in almost any other role that I can think of doing.*

**This is Sam's story.**

*My first job, eleven years ago, was with a market research company. We used to work odd hours and frequently away from home, which was great, particularly for a new graduate. We also got paid overtime and bonuses for being away which was even better. What was not so good was HR. We filled in a time sheet every week which was copied to a master spreadsheet and then HR calculated our wages. Every month they got it wrong. Too much, too little, never the right amount. It was really frustrating.*

*However, over time, the work that I was doing did not really change, we did the same things each year, so I started to look for a new role where I could use my degree and also learn new skills. When I learnt about PayDay, it was clear to me why it was so useful. I knew how frustrating it was to get paid incorrectly every month and PayDay eliminates many of these problems. I really enjoy getting out and meeting people and helping people to solve problems that I have had in the past, it means a lot more to me.*

**Exercise – why do you do what you do?**

Answer each of these questions and then build a short story that tells your customer how you got to where you are now. You do not have to include all of the details that you write out.

When did you start this role?


What were you doing before this role?


What was the trigger for ending that?


What made you want to do this current role?


What inspires you?


What is it about the product that you sell that that excites you?


Why are you different?


This is why I do what I do.

## CUSTOMER RESEARCH

If your customer is going to trust you, you must be credible. This means that you have to know something about them before you ever go to see them. The primary purpose of this research is to ensure that they have the potential to be a customer. For example, to be a customer of TRIC Software, a company needs to have its own HR department. If this is outsourced, then the company is very unlikely to manage its own payroll so is unlikely to require software to do this.

There will be certain characteristics of a company that define if they are likely to be a customer for you. These are important things to determine before you ever see them. You should make a list of these things.

When doing your research, it is also helpful to find out basic information about what the company is doing, reviewing its news or press releases so that you are aware of the bigger picture beyond their need for your product.

**Example - What Sam wants to know about a customer**

For TRIC Software, these are the things that are important for Sam to find out about a potential customer.

1. How many employees does the customer have?

2. Where are they located? (headquarters and other offices)

3. Does it already run applications in the cloud?

4. Is there a payroll specialist employed in HR?

5. Do they have irregular or complicated employee payments?

6. Are they an existing customer of TRIC Software?

7. Does TRIC Software have existing customers who do similar work who might have had similar issues as the target customer?

8. Do they outsource lots of processes or like to keep things internal?

9. What accounting software do they use?

Sam will not be able to find all of this information without asking the company. However, it is important information to learn as early as possible in the sales process.

**Exercise – What Do you want to know about a customer?**

List the most important things that you would like to know about your customers. Rank them in order of priority. Try to give an indication of where you may be able to find this information.

1.

2.

3.

4.

5.

6.

7.

8.

9.

10.

## WHAT DOES A GOOD CUSTOMER LOOK LIKE?

It is highly unlikely that your company has sufficient sales resources to fully target every possible customer equally. It is also likely that not every company will be interested in your product at the same time. As a result, you have to prioritise your work and focus on the customers that are most likely to buy your product in the near future.

For TRIC Software, Sam has defined some criteria for a good customer for PayDay. These are:

- Payroll is an in-house function, not outsourced.

- They have multiple offices / countries and / or irregular or complicated payment schedules?

- They have a large number of employees

- They run applications in the cloud already.

- Their headquarters are close to Leicester

- They are an existing customer of their other software

- Sam's knows someone who works there or has access to decision makers

Based on this, Sam then builds a table to evaluate potential customers.

*The Equation of Sales*

| Criteria | Poor | | Good | | Comment | Score | Action | |
|---|---|---|---|---|---|---|---|---|
| Payroll is in-house | No | 1 | Yes | 10 | | | | |
| Multiple offices etc | No | 1 | Yes | 10 | | | | |
| Number of employees | Less than 100 | 1 | More than 1000 | 10 | | | | |
| Applications in the cloud | No | 2 | Yes | 5 | | | | |
| HQ near Leicester | More than 100m away | 1 | Less than 10m away | 5 | | | | |
| Existing customer | No | 2 | Yes | 4 | | | | |
| Easy contact | No | 2 | Yes | 4 | | | | |

| Criteria | Poor | | Good | | Comment | Score | Action |
|---|---|---|---|---|---|---|---|
| Payroll is in-house | No | 1 | Yes | 10 | Yes, they employee a specialist | 10 | |
| Multiple offices etc | No | 1 | Yes | 10 | No, just one office | 1 | |
| Number of employees | Less than 100 | 1 | More than 1000 | 10 | About 500 | 5 | |
| Applications in the cloud | No | 2 | Yes | 5 | No | 2 | Send information on the advantages of working in the cloud |
| HQ near Leicester | More than 100m away | 1 | Less than 10m away | 5 | In Birmingham, 43m away | 3 | |
| Existing customer | No | 2 | Yes | 4 | No | 2 | |
| Easy contact | No | 2 | Yes | 4 | John in HR | 4 | |

Each customer is then ranked based on this table. For example, this is the scoring for one company.

This customer scores 27 out a possible 48 points. There is not a lot that Sam can do about most of the criteria where the customer does not match the best score. Sam has no influence over the number of offices or staff that the company has. However, Sam can limit the issue that they have not deployed applications in the cloud before by educating them about the advantages of working in the cloud as part of the sales process.

Think about what factors make your customers better or worse. Not all of them will be equally important so you will have to rank them. You can then analyse each customer against each of the factors to compare customers against each other.

You may have to do this exercise by country and by product line as the ranking may vary for each.

This is also an exercise that you should repeat on a regular basis. I suggest every six months. While the initial analysis might be time consuming, the reviews take much less time.

Use the ranking to focus on which customers to prioritise for the next period of activity. Try to complete the actions that you have defined to improve the scoring of customers.

**Example – This is how Sam ranks customers**

| What do they do? | Why is this valuable? | Ranking |
|---|---|---|
| Payroll is an in-house function, not outsourced. | If it is outsourced, then they do not need an in-house software product | 1 |
| Do they have multiple offices / countries and/or irregular or complicated payment schedules? | The more complicated payroll is, the more issues they are likely to have which PayDay can solve | 2 |
| What is the total number of employees? The bigger the better! | Revenue is proportional to the number. | 3 |
| Do they run applications in the cloud already? | If they do, then it is easier to persuade them to use another in the cloud. | 4 |
| Distance from Leicester – the smaller the better. | Sam has to travel to each customer so the further the distance, the longer the journey | 5 |
| Are they an existing customer? | It is always easier to sell to an existing customer. | 6 |
| Do we know someone there or have an easy route to meet the decision makers? | This prevents the need for a cold call. | 7 |

**Exercise – What are the characteristics of your good customer?**

List all of the positive characteristics of your best customers; indicate why they are valuable to you and rank them in order of importance.

| What do they do? | Why is this valuable? | Ranking |
|---|---|---|
|  |  |  |
|  |  |  |
|  |  |  |
|  |  |  |
|  |  |  |
|  |  |  |
|  |  |  |

Now use this to build a ranking for all of your customers and determine your best ones.

## HOW TO GET THROUGH THE FRONT DOOR

The hardest thing any sales person ever has to sell is their initial contact. Most people are too busy and focussed on what they have to do today to take notice of a new contact. Even when you call them directly, they will typically choose to reject the approach. This is not because they do not have problems or that they are not interested, they just do not understand why they should be interested.

You need to construct an opening for each customer that attracts their attention and makes them want to speak to you. There are two parts to this:

1. Introduction / please don't put the phone down (30 seconds)

2. Here's why you should arrange to meet with me (2 minutes)

Part One should be something like this:

"Hi, I'm_____" (your name)

"From _____" (company)

"We help _____" (type of customer)

"To_____" (do what?)

Faster / cheaper / safer

"By_____" (how?)

"Do you have a couple of minutes for a chat?"

Part Two should be something like this:

"This is a typical problem for companies like yours"

"This is our solution"

"Can we talk?"

**Example - Sam's Opening Statements**

Hi, I'm Sam from TRIC Software. We help medium to large sized businesses to save time and money using integrated HR software for a variety of functions including payroll. Do you have a couple of minutes to have a quick chat?"

After a positive response, Sam follows up with a series of questions such as:

"In employee surveys, 90% of employees agree or strongly agree that getting their wages paid correctly on the right day was very important to them. Is this something that you would agree with?"

"Despite this, 60% of companies acknowledge that they make mistakes each month as a result of their complicated payroll process and that the effort to correct it is long and painful. Is this something that you are familiar with?"

"TRIC Software's product, PayDay, is trusted by over 1000 companies to get payroll right first time, every month and we can demonstrate that it can reduce errors in payroll by over 90% within 3 months of implementation. Is this something that you might be interested to learn more about?"

**Exercise – How to Get through the front Door**

What information do you have that your customer does not know but would be of value to them?

What might a customer be missing out on that you can help them with?

How have your products helped similar businesses to improve their productivity?

Do you have a customer success story that you can tell?

Plan an opening statement to a potential customer for when they answer the phone and if you need to leave a message. The message should tempt them enough to call you back.

**SCIENCE OF PERSUASION**

The Science of Persuasion consists of six ideas that can help you to persuade others to do what you would like them to do. Given that sales is all about persuading people to buy your product, these ideas are well worth reviewing. They are:

1. Reciprocity – Give before you receive;

2. Scarcity - People want more of those things that they can have less of;

3. Authority - People follow the lead of creditable, knowledgeable experts;

4. Consistency - Looking for commitments that can be made;

5. Liking - People who are similar to us;

6. Consensus – Doing what others are doing.

You may want to review the video on YouTube, "Secrets from the Science of Persuasion" https://www.youtube.com/watch?v=cFdCzN7RYbw.

**Example - TRIC Software and Sam regularly do the following for their customers**

1. Sam brings blueberry muffins to the first meeting with a new customer. (Reciprocity)

2. TRIC Software has a finite number of implementation consultants so when Sam needs to get a quick decision, the potential scarcity of these resources is usually mentioned. (Scarcity)

3. TRIC Software annually runs a salary survey of all of its customers and distributes the results free of charge to all participants. This allows customers to benchmark themselves against similar companies to ensure that they are paying competitive salaries. (Reciprocity)

4. TRIC Software has an annual user group meeting where customers are encouraged to present how they are getting benefit from their implementations. (Consensus)

5. When a customer has made a particularly significant improvement to their processes, Sam creates a video success story which is posted on LinkedIn, YouTube and TRIC Software website and circulated to other customers. (Consensus)

**Exercise – what can you do to persuade your customers?**

Based on the science of persuasion, what can you do with/for your customers that will develop your powers of persuasion?

1. Reciprocity – Give before you receive;

2. Scarcity - People want more of those things that they can have less of;

3. Authority - People follow the lead of creditable, knowledgeable experts;

4. Consistency - Looking for commitments that can be made;

5. Liking - People who are similar to us;

6. Consensus – Doing what others are doing.


Try to define five actions that you can do on a permanent basis to make to more likely that your customer will say yes.

1.


2.


3.


4.


5.

## NEEDS ANALYSIS

I believe that no business buys something that they do not need. It is the role of the sales person to identify those needs, propose a solution that involves their products and then get the customer to want those products. As a result, identifying those needs is the most important thing that a sales person does.

A very simple workflow that generates a sale can be defined as:

1. Customer is doing process A

2. During process A, customer encounters a problem that prevents its completion

3. Customer buys product from supplier to solve the problem

4. Customer successfully completes process A.

The task of product managers and sales people is to identify all of the possible processes that a customer is doing that might result in them buying the particular product that they are offering. Ask yourself the questions:

1. What might a company be doing to make them need to buy your product?

2. What are they going to do once they have access to the product?

| Feature | Possible event to create a need |
|---|---|
| It runs in the cloud | Company is migrating other processes to cloud-based software. Company is opening a second office and the cloud will remove the need for additional computing infrastructure. |
| Tax and benefit rules are automatically updated | Company is advertising for a tax and benefits specialist to come to work for them. |

| Integrates with accounting software | Company has just implemented new accounting software or is ending such an agreement. |
|---|---|
| Management dashboard | Management has announced a major review of operations and costs. |

For example, these are some of the features of PayDay. For each, Sam has identified an event that might suggest that a customer might be developing a need for the product.

Sam is therefore able to look out for such triggers and, when one presents itself, will immediately approach a company to discuss in more detail.

These can be difficult to think of initially. Start by thinking of the things that you would like to know about a customer. Then start to think about the things that might change which would make them want your product. It may help to review Chapter 15, Why Change, when thinking about this.

**Example – Evidence of Potential Needs**

When looking for new customers, Sam looks for evidence that they might be interested in using PayDay. Sam knows that all companies must have some system for calculating salary but Sam needs more than that to justify a call. Sam knows that no company advertises its errors in payroll so needs to look for clues about their needs rather than definitive statements. These are some of the things that Sam looks for.

- A company announces that they are adopting a different cloud-based system in another part of its business.

- An organisation is advertising for a payroll specialist. A new hire is often open to change.

- An organisation is looking to expand either by opening a new office or hiring many more staff.

- An organisation has many part-time staff.

- An organisation that has a mixture of staff that get paid on a weekly or monthly basis.

Sam is also a member of various payroll related groups on LinkedIn and regularly monitors posts to search for companies who are not happy with their existing payroll software supplier.

**Exercise – why might a customer need your product?**

What might a company be doing to make them buy your product?

What are they going to do once they have bought it?

Try to be as granular as possible.

## VALUE SELLING

While sales people sell products, customers buy value. This is possibly the most important thing for any sales person to remember. Unless you can define the value of your product to a customer, then they are going to struggle to understand why they should buy it. As the saying goes, "Value is not determined by those who set the price. Value is determined by those who choose to pay it."

In this exercise, you need to list all the features and functions of your product and define why they are a benefit a customer. Remember that if you can still say "so what?", then you have not defined a benefit. You will typically only use the best three of four benefits for any one client and will need to select the most appropriate from this list.

## Example – Payday's features and benefits

| Feature | Why is this useful to the customer? |
|---|---|
| It runs in the cloud | Customer can access from anywhere on any device which saves time. There is no need for any customer staff to support it or manage upgrades which saves money. |
| Tax and benefit rules are automatically updated | This saves time as the company does not have to keep track of these changes and determine their impact. |
| Integrates with accounting software | Credits and debits are automatically recorded in accounts improving the process and saving time. |
| Manages all aspects of pay in a single package | This reduces the risk of error and avoids upsetting staff. It also saves time and money. |
| It automatically emails payslips to employees | This ensures that all staff receive their payslip on the correct day and saves time on having to distribute the payslips and saves on resources from not having to print them. |
| Management dashboard | Management can review and model changes based on the most accurate data enabling them to better manage the business. |
| Links to banking software | Automatic payments direct to staff, further reducing time to process payments, saving time and money. |

**Exercise – What are the features and benefits of your solution?**

| Feature | Why is this useful to the customer? |
|---------|-------------------------------------|
|         |                                     |
|         |                                     |
|         |                                     |
|         |                                     |
|         |                                     |
|         |                                     |
|         |                                     |

Remember that if you can still say "so what?", then you have not defined a benefit. You will typically only use the best three or four benefits for any one client and will need to select the most appropriate from this list.

## WHY CHANGE?

Studies have shown that up to 60% of sales opportunities are lost to "no decision" rather than competitors. In these instances, the companies decide to do nothing rather than do something. This may seem strange as they clearly believed at some point that they needed a new product or they had a problem that had to be fixed yet they chose to do nothing about it.

The simple fact is that without a compelling case for change, companies will tend to do nothing. Most companies "already have something that does that". For example, if they are in business to manufacture something, then they generally already have the means of production. It may not be big enough or fast enough but it does what is required.

As a result, in order to generate an opportunity, a customer has to understand the opposite view. What is the risk of doing nothing? How much better will life be if they do decide to proceed? Without a clear understanding of the risk of doing nothing or a compelling vision of "what better looks like", customers will tend to do nothing. Imagine if they do not implement a time saving process and they lose customers and have to make cutbacks to survive. This is not something that any business wants so the risk of not proceeding is higher than the risk of implementing the new process.

Without a clear vision of "what better looks like", customers will tend to do nothing so you may have to persuade them to change. What can you say that may push them out of their comfort zone and into the window of dissatisfaction. The reasons will generally be associated with one of the following:

- Technology
- Customer needs
- The Economy
- Competition
- Government Regulations

*Examples and Exercises*

**Example – Sam will often include these facts in discussions with customers**

Companies that have migrated their payroll processes to the cloud typically save 20% of the time for payroll compared to using desktop or standalone applications.

Millennials working in corporations expect to be able to have instant access to data from anywhere.

Government introduces new regulations or changes to regulations seven to eight times per year on average. Each time, this requires you to change your payroll processes. They do not always widely publicise these changes so companies that manage their own payroll have to continually monitor government websites for such changes and then implement them. We estimate that this takes one month per year.

Online banking has been used by 90% of companies for the last five years and in recent surveys, 80% of people stated that they trusted that this information is securely held. PayDay adheres to all of the same standards as online banking so is just as secure.

Please note. These are not hard facts! They are used to illustrate the point rather than being absolutely accurate.

207

**Exercise – What factors might make your customer want to change?**

What can you say to move your customer from "status quo" to the "window of dissatisfaction"?

What technology might be available to make them change?

What has changed with your customer's customer?

What economic changes are happening that will influence them?

What new competitors are there? What are they doing that is different?

What regulations have been implemented in the last 6-12 months that impact them?

## WHY ARE YOU UNIQUE?

Having established that the customer wants to change, we now have to persuade them that they must choose your product. If you are the person to persuade a company to change, you are in pole position to sell them your solution. However, even then, companies may want to shop around or they may already be looking for alternatives by the time that you talk to them. It is unusual for you to be the only possible option for them to choose. As a result, you may have to persuade your customer to choose your product rather than the competition. To do that, you have to focus on the uniqueness of your product.

Think about all of the things that makes your company or your products unique? Then, define why these should matter to your potential customer. Highlight those that are most unique and most valuable to the customer. These are the best ideas.

Uniqueness is defined by:

- Only one (or very few) copies exist.
- An item is limited by situation or geography
- It may have a unique product or no equal.

You may have to consider just small elements of your product to be unique rather than the whole thing.

**Example – What Makes PayDay Unique?**

TRIC Software understands that there is a lot of competition for
payroll technology and that differentiation via the technology is
extremely difficult.   While it is possible to define some specific
uniquenesses for individual customers, they tend to promote their
uniqueness through the value added services that they offer.

| TRIC Software unique offerings | Why does this matter to the customer? |
|---|---|
| Salary survey of all PayDay customers.  This is provided as a free service to all customers. | This ensures that customers pay their staff competitive salaries which helps to retain staff, to hire new staff and reduce the cost of hiring. |
| User Group Meeting, offered to all customers. | This gives customers the chance to learn from other customers who are using the software on a day to day basis. |
| Tax and benefit specialists | This provides free information to customers plus support for customers who do not have such expertise in-house. |
| Success stories | For customers who participate in these, they have the chance to demonstrate to their customers how successful they are and how they are saving time and money. |

**Exercise– What makes your Product unique?**

| Why is your company / product unique? | Why does your customer care about this? |
|---|---|
|  |  |
|  |  |
|  |  |
|  |  |
|  |  |
|  |  |
|  |  |
|  |  |

## WHAT DOES A GOOD OPPORTUNITY LOOK LIKE?

Every sales person that I know has spent time chasing after a sale that never happened. Sales people are frequently very competitive and will spend time chasing all opportunities hoping to win them all. That can result in a lot of wasted time and effort that could have been better spent elsewhere. In the same way that not every customer is a good customer today, not every opportunity is worth pursuing.

By focussing on the best opportunities, you are more likely to be more successful and make more money. There will be a variety of criteria that you might use to determine the value of an opportunity.

These criteria could include:

- How much revenue will we make?
- Are all the different buyers known?
- Is the budget known and understood?
- Have we worked with this customer previously?
- Are we the vendor that most matches their needs?
- How strong is the competition?
- How does our product fit with their existing infrastructure?

Once we have identified all of the different criteria, we have to have a way of managing all of them so that more important criteria are given a greater weight. To that end, we have to determine which factors determine how valuable each opportunity is and then how important each of these factors is. To do this, we use the table below.

| Criteria | What is the criteria? |
|---|---|
| Poor | What does a poor opportunity look like? What score does that equate to? |
| Good | What does a good opportunity look like? What score does that equate to? |
| Score | What score will you assign to this opportunity? |
| Comment | What is the reason for this score |

| Action | What can you do to improve this score? |
|--------|----------------------------------------|
|        |                                        |

Start by identifying the criteria that determine what a good opportunity looks like. Then rank all of the criteria from most to least important. This will then let you assign the relative scores to each criterion.

Once you have done that, you can start to rank all of your opportunities.

**Example – Sam's Good Opportunity management system**

For Sam, a good opportunity analysis is very similar to a good customer analysis as there are few opportunities to add revenue from an existing customer apart from the customer increasing staff numbers, something which Sam has no control over. In ranking opportunities, Sam primarily uses the good customer analysis to focus on which opportunities to chase.

Sam refines the analysis to include the following:

| Criteria | Why is this important? | Ranking |
|---|---|---|
| Buyers Identified | Has each been met and are needs well understood | 1 |
| Budget know and available | Does it match the size of the deal, including implementation costs | 2 |
| Growth potential | Is the customer planning to expand, in which case, future revenues will increase | 3 |
| Ease of implementation | A difficult implementation is expensive and lengthy and it is difficult to persuade the customer to bear all of the costs involved. | 4 |
| Can this opportunity open doors elsewhere? | If this deal closes, can it be used as an example to help to persuade other customers to follow | 5 |

**Exercise – What makes a good opportunity?**

| Criteria | Why is this important to you? | Ranking |
|---|---|---|
|  |  |  |
|  |  |  |
|  |  |  |
|  |  |  |
|  |  |  |
|  |  |  |
|  |  |  |

# Extras

# REFERENCES

(*) The Quote in the dedication comes from "Born to Run" by Bruce Springsteen – a song guaranteed to cheer me up regardless of the circumstances.

Geert Hofstede, Gert Jan Hofstede, Michael Minkov, "Cultures and Organizations, Software of the Mind", Third Revised Edition, McGrawHill 2010, ISBN 0-07-166418-1. www.geerthofstede.com. ©Geert Hofstede B.V. quoted with permission.

https://www.amazon.co.uk/Cultures-Organizations-Intercultural-Cooperation-Importance/dp/0071664181

Amy Cuddy, (2015) "Presence: Bringing Your Boldest Self to Your Biggest Challenges"

https://www.amazon.co.uk/Presence-Bringing-Boldest-Biggest-Challenges/dp/0316256579

Rachel Botsman, (2017) "Who Can You Trust?"

https://www.amazon.co.uk/Who-Can-You-Trust-Technology/dp/024129617X

Mike Adams (2018). "Seven Stories Every Salesperson Must Tell"

https://www.amazon.co.uk/Seven-Stories-Every-Salesperson-Must/dp/1925648699/

Steven Johnson (2011). "Where Good Ideas Come From: The Seven Patterns of Innovation".

https://www.amazon.co.uk/Where-Good-Ideas-Come-Innovation/dp/0141033401

Charles Darwin (2009). The Expression of the Emotions in Man and Animals

https://www.amazon.co.uk/Expression-Emotions-Animals-Penguin-Classics/dp/0141439440

Alison Brooks and Leslie John (2018). "The Surprising Power of Questions". Harvard Business Review.

https://hbr.org/2018/05/the-surprising-power-of-questions

Geoffrey Moore (2014) "Crossing the Chasm"
https://www.amazon.co.uk/Crossing-Chasm-3rd-Disruptive-Mainstream/dp/0062292986

Peter Kraljic (1983). "Purchasing Must Become Supply Management" Harvard Business Review https://hbr.org/1983/09/purchasing-must-become-supply-management.

Paddi Lund (various). http://www.paddilund.com/

- Teams -- Building the Happiness Centred Business – highly recommended
- Credibility -- The Absolutely Critical Non-Essentials
- Marketing -- Training Customers to Treasure Your Business –
- Customer Care -- Simply Stunning Customer Service
- Money -- The Secret of Customers Who Love to Pay
- Advertising -- Mobilising Your Customer Sales Force

Jack Zenger and Joseph Folkman (2016) "What Great Listeners Actually Do".

https://hbr.org/2016/07/what-great-listeners-actually-do

David G. Pugh and Terry R. Bacon (2005). Powerful Proposals.

https://www.amazon.co.uk/Powerful-Proposals-Give-Business-Winning/dp/081447232X

Maslow's Hierarchy of Needs.
https://www.simplypsychology.org/maslow.html#gsc.tab=0

# LIST OF FIGURES

**LIST OF TABLES**

## GLOSSARY OF TERMS

For anyone who is new to sales, some of the terminology can be a little daunting. As this book has been written for people who are relatively new to sales, it is useful to have a set of definitions to work with.

| | |
|---|---|
| Inside Sales | This is where customers are encouraged to make the initial connection to a company and talk to a sales person on the phone. This sales person is generally referred to as working on Inside Sales |
| Outside / Direct Sales | This is where the sales person usually makes the first contact with the customer to generate interest in a product, followed by visiting the customer's office. |
| Business to Business (B2B) | This is where one business sells directly to another business |
| Business to Consumer (B2C) | This is where a business sells directly to a single person |
| Business Development | This is the sales activity that is done to generate new customers or promote a new product. |
| Account Management | This is the work done to manage and sell to existing customers |
| Agency Sales | This is where a company does not have their own sales team but employs a series of agents to sell for them. The agent will frequently represent a number of different companies. |
| Consultative Selling | This is a style of selling that focuses on building trust with the customer to understand their needs before recommending a specific product or service. |
| eCommerce | This is selling directly through a website. It requires sales and marketing effort to encourage the customer to visit the site. |

| Vertical market | This is a product that is sold to a very specific industry and is almost never used outside of that industry. |
|---|---|
| Horizontal market | This is a product that can be sold to any company regardless of the industry that they are working in. |
| CRM | Customer Relationship Management. Software used to store customer contacts and opportunities. |
| Perpetual Software License | Customers only ever have a license to use software, they do not own software. A perpetual license is owned by the customer and lasts forever. |
| Subscription or Leased License | This is a license that is paid for periodically, usually annually, and is never owned by the customer. |

BV - #0003 - 291123 - C24 - 229/152/13 - PB - 9781913839192 - Gloss Lamination